Charlotte Mary Yonge

Bye-Words

a collection of tales, new and old

Charlotte Mary Yonge

Bye-Words
a collection of tales, new and old

ISBN/EAN: 9783337023768

Printed in Europe, USA, Canada, Australia, Japan

Cover: Foto ©Thomas Meinert / pixelio.de

More available books at **www.hansebooks.com**

BYE-WORDS

BYE-WORDS

A COLLECTION OF TALES

NEW AND OLD

BY

CHARLOTTE M. YONGE

AUTHOR OF 'THE HEIR OF REDCLYFFE' ETC

London
MACMILLAN AND CO.
AND NEW YORK
1889

First Edition 1879
Reprinted 1889

PREFACE.

SOME OF THESE TALES in illustration of proverbs and bye-words have previously appeared, the others see the light for the first time. All the historical ones are intended to describe what might have been rather than what actually was, except 'Buy a Broom,' which is founded on one of the many stories of the adventures of Charles V. in disguise.

'Our Ghost at Fantford,' 'Anna's Wedding Cake,' and even 'Patty Applecheeks,' all have a certain slight foundation in fact.

C. M. YONGE.

November 6, 1879.

CONTENTS.

	PAGE
THE BOY BISHOP	1
ONE WILL AND THREE WAYS	39
KASPAR'S SUMMER DREAM	81
BUY A BROOM	125
THE TRAVELS OF TWO KITS	185
SELMA'S SECRET SIGHS	229
OUR GHOST AT FANTFORD	257
ANNA'S WEDDING CAKE	273
AUTOBIOGRAPHY OF PATTY APPLECHEEKS	285
A HOLIDAY ENGAGEMENT; OR, THE CAMPBELLS ARE COMING	309

THE BOY BISHOP.

To ilka blade of grass its ain drap o' dew.

CHAPTER I.

FOUR hundred and seventy years count for little in the history of those huge circles of enormous stones that stand mysteriously upon Salisbury Plain. Their massive triplets rose in the same strange loneliness then as now, and cast the selfsame strange shadows as they barred the light of the September sun, whose low beams, coming from the east, made all the Down one glancing, sparkling frosted sheet of dew, netted over with countless diamond-hung lines of gossamer strung from one bent to another.

The stones—perhaps a little more complete and with a few more stones lying across the top of their supporters—struck the eye with wonder as they do still, but the explanation given to the traveller was uttered much more unhesitatingly. 'Those stones, my Lord? They are the same which the great wizard Merlin brought in one night from Africa at the bidding of King Vortigern, by art magic. From which the saints defend us!' Wherewith Sir Martin, the Parson of Ambresbury, or Amesbury, crossed himself.

He was riding among a numerous cavalcade of

clergy and their attendants, in close attendance upon a slightly-made man, with a keen, thoughtful, refined face, wrapped in a dark robe lined with lamb's skin, whose hood covered his shaven head. His cross-bearer and the other chief attendants were some way in the rear, riding at ease until they should enter some village or town, when the Church bells would ring, and they would form into procession, as befitted the new Bishop, Robert Hallam, making his first visitation of his diocese. He had slept at Amesbury, and was on his way to his Cathedral, where he was to be welcomed with all due pomp and splendour. His reply was, 'So have I read in the "Chronicles of Geoffrey of Monmouth." Shall we lose too much time if we view them nearer?'

'Your Lordship's way lies not far from them,' returned the priest, who was convoying him; 'and by this fair rising sun, in such holy company, methinks no ill can befall; but the stones have an ill-fame, my Lord. They were brought hither by magic, and it is said that on yonder altar-stone offerings of men were made, and that their spirits yet haunt the place.'

'Yea,' added the Bishop's secretary, who rode not far off, a young scholar from Oxford, 'it was there that foul slaughter was done upon the Britons by Henghist, wherefore they be called Stone Heng—the stones of Henghist! Hark!'

'They moan still!' exclaimed the fat sumpnour. 'Go no farther, my Lord.'

'Nay, if such poor spirits be in bondage here, it were well to enquire whether they may be released,' said the Bishop. 'How say you, Master Dixon?'

'I say,' replied the secretary, smiling, that the spirits must be near akin to the Egyptian stone that made sweet music when the morning sunbeams played upon it—'

For a sweet childish voice was heard coming as it were out of the midst of the circle of stones. The sumpnour crossed himself, and an awe-struck whisper went round. 'They moan and gibber.'

'No ill spirit walks after sunrise,' said the chaplain reprovingly.

'Nor singeth such joyous noels,' added the Bishop. 'Hearken again!'

And this time there was no doubt that it was a clear, childish voice that was singing sweetly, with joyous, ringing notes the quaint old carol—

> 'The moon shone bright, and the stars gave a light,
>   A little before it was day;
> Our Lord, our God, He called on us,
>   And bade us awake and pray.
> The fields were green as green could be,
>   When from His glorious seat
> Our Lord, our God, He watered us
>   With His heavenly dew so sweet.'

Pushing forward a little on his mule, Bishop Hallam saw, as though framed by three massive stones, a number of sheep, the low sun lighting on their woolly backs as they browsed on the short grass within the mystic circle, and seated on the very altar-stone itself, their little shepherd, the singer, his fair hair glancing in the morning sun, and his little crook in his hand, all unknowing that he was observed, as with the joyous unconsciousness of the birds themselves, he poured forth his sweet notes of song.

The Bishop made a motion with his hand to hinder any interruption, and his eyes filled with tears as he whispered to his chaplain the Latin words, ' "The weaned child shall put his hand on the cockatrice den." I thank Heaven for such a sparkling dew-drop of the morning of my episcopate!'

By this time a rough-looking dog had run up from the opposite side of the circle, and begun to bark. The little shepherd broke off his song and turned, much amazed at the various dark figures he saw invading his solitude.

'Come hither, my child,' called the Bishop, as the face, fair-featured and rosy with true Saxon beauty, was turned towards him. 'Come hither, and tell me thy name.'

'I see who it is,' said Sir Martin. 'It is the child who herds the sheep of the nunnery at Amesbury.

His mother, a widow, died in the hospitium, and the Sisters have fed and clothed him, and bred him up at their porter's lodge. Make thine obedience, boy; this is the Lord Bishop.'

The child, with a readiness that did credit to the nurture of the good nuns, came forward, bared his fair flaxen head, kneeling down for the blessing of the Bishop.

'What is thy name, my fair child?' asked Hallam when he had blessed him with uplifted hand.

'Oswald, an it please your reverence,' replied the little fellow, who seemed about nine years old, and looked up with a face as winning as it was fair.

'Who taught thee to sing so sweetly?'

'The good Sisters,' shyly answered the boy.

'They taught thee whatever thou knowest, I'll be sworn,' said Sir Martin. 'How art thou not afraid to be all alone in the midst of the Wizard's stones? Not another lad would dare feed his flock there?'

The boy's bright blue eyes were full of a sort of amused wonder as he simply said, 'I crossed me.'

'Thou art right, my son,' said the Bishop. 'There is nothing in these heathen stones to hurt a Christian child who does his duty well and singeth such goodly songs. So the good Sisters have taught thee to sing? Knowest thou thy Credo?'

The boy, with feet close together, stood straight

up and rehearsed the Creed in the strange form to which tradition had reduced the Latin. Yet it had a musical sweetness of cadence, and the Bishop found he likewise knew the English version.

'It is well, my fair child,' said Bishop Robert. 'Here is a silver groat for thee, and thou mayst tell the good Lady Prioress that the new shepherd doth bless and thank her for so tending a lamb of his flock.'

'Yea,' he added, as he rode on, 'it is a sight I thank God for. Would that I may tend my flock as carefully, if not as blithesomely, as yonder little child in the morning sunshine!'

'Poor child,' said another of the Amesbury clergy, 'I trow he seeks the spot because none of the other herd boys dare enter the ring of magic stones, and he is safe from being mocked and jeered at as my Lady Prioress' messan dog, when he will not share in their ill-doings.'

'It were well,' said the Chaplain, 'to have so goodly a voice in your Lordship's choir.'

'Cage the singing-bird, quotha?' returned the Bishop. 'Were that a good deed?'

'So please you, my Lord, I think it were,' said the Parson of Amesbury. 'As Brother Giles hath been telling me, the child hath been somewhat cockered by the good Sisters, to whom he hath been a right pleasant toy, as a cosset lamb might be, ever since his mother came dying to their door. Now, even like the lamb, he hath grown too big for a nun's toy, and they wot not what to do with him. They have of late sent him out with their sheep, and put him to the like acts of service; but he is tenderly nurtured, and of a meek and godly frame, so that the lads of his own degree flout and chase him, till he is fain to hide himself from them in the Wizard's ring, where none of them will enter.'

'Yea,' added Brother Giles, as the Bishop's look of enquiry rested on him, 'it is but a few days since that the Lady Prioress spake to me of her care on his account, and asked whether he could not find a place in some chapel; or even become a scholar at St. Mary's at Winchester. He hath good gifts, and might well rise, even like the Lord Archbishop himself, from being a shepherd on the Downs to being a shepherd of men.'

'Ah well!' said the Bishop. 'It might seem pity to take the shepherd lad from his hills of glistening dew to the dust and clamour of cities, but it seems there are perils for him even here. If the Prioress will let him go, let us ask for him, and strive that at least the dew of Grace be never withdrawn or parched up from him!'

CHAPTER II.

'Is it well to license this children's procession?' said Bishop Robert Hallam to the Dean of his Cathedral, as they paced up and down the cloistered walk, in the alternate light and shadow of its arches.

'The common folk will be much displeased if it be hindered another year,' returned the Dean. 'They claim it as their right in all Cathedral Churches, and as your reverent Lordship well knows, there is a special rite provided for it in the great book of the holy Saint Osmond himself, proper to our own Cathedral of New Sarum.'

'True,' replied Bishop Robert. 'The custom was devised by some pious man to show how truly out of the mouths of babes and sucklings might come forth praise; but what with the naughtiness of childhood, and the lewdness of the people, and far more the neglect of the clergy, it may become a mere day of profane ribaldry, even within the sanctuary.'

'Even so,' returned the Dean. 'They deem it

their day of license. The last Childermas Day, when the *Episcopus Puerorum* came in procession, the rabble spread through the whole building. They sat in the stalls, and sang profane songs. One of the best stoles was lost, four windows cracked, an arm of St. Edward's image was broken, and the tail of St. Margaret's dragon; one woman was trodden to death, and two men fought with staves at the west door so hotly that a lay brother who tried to part them, got his hand maimed for life; more than a score of purses were cut in the scuffle; I myself stumbled over a man lying in a dead drunken fit by this very cloister door that same night, and the foulness and filth that were left were such that the sacristan had to borrow six lay brothers to help in the cleansing. Since that we have tried to stave off such a day of riot. One winter there was a fever in the town, the next there was a flood, such that the water came half-way up the pillars in the nave, then came the death of the last Bishop; and from one cause or another we have contrived to hinder it; but now, as I am told, the townsfolk declare they will no longer see their children baulked of their lawful sport, and if we take not the lead, and cause the Boy Bishop to be elected from among our own choristers, they will make one of their own, burst into the Cathedral, and there will be nought but mad revelry and ribaldry.'

'We have a right, then, Master Dean, to elect our own chorister-bishop?'

'Aye, my Lord. By the statutes he must be one of the choristers, who hath sung long in the Church, and is also handsome and wellformed in face and limb. No other choice is valid. Moreover in the twelfth year of King Edward the Second, it was ordained that the *Episcopus Puerorum* should make no feast, since such tended only to riot and debauchery.'

'Then,' said the Bishop, 'we must do our best to turn the feast to edification, as the good men designed who intended it! Methinks we have one child in the choir who will not only fulfil the statute by his fairness of face and limb, but will lead the holy song with a heart full of praise, and do his best to hinder any profanity.'

'Your Lordship means little Oswald of Amesbury,' said the Dean. 'He is a fair and towardly child, and hath a sweet voice, though he be not quick of wit. Moreover being a lone orphan, he is the more suitable, as none will have claims upon him. Your Lordship is aware that any benefice in your gift which falls vacant between the feast of St. Nicolas and Childermas Day, is at the bestowal of the Boy Bishop.'

'So I had heard.'

'Indeed,' added the Dean, 'I was credibly told that much of this vehemence on the part of the commonalty was the work of Denis, the Fletcher, in the hope that his son Diccon may play the part of Bishop, and bestow any preferment there may be to give on his brother Piers, a fellow whom, for his evil life and rude brawls, we had to cast out from the choir some years since, and who hath since—as I hear—become a begging friar, and goeth his rounds as a pardoner.'

'This Diccon is a chorister, I think,' said the Bishop. 'A black-browed lad—not ill-favoured, save that he hath a scowl—and with a good voice, if he would pay heed to what he is doing, and would not sing as though he were in an ale-house.'

'The very lad, my Lord. If he were chosen, only mischief could ensue; and yet if he be not chosen, his father may belike work even worse harm.'

'Worse he cannot work,' said Hallam, 'than the profanity it would be in us to entrust the leading of such holy rites to a lad like Diccon, who as yet knows nought of holy fear, and would make them a mere jest. See, Master Dean, this shall be what we will do. We will gather the children of the choir in the Chapter-house, and I will there speak to them, and make them understand the meaning of the service. After which we will cause the most meet to be elected, and endeavour our utmost that the day shall be to the glory of God, and not to His dishonour.'

The Dean agreed, for Bishop Hallam was not a man to be gainsaid, and moreover had a power of infusing something of his own spirit into those whom he addressed. Hitherto the Chapter had been wont to think of the Procession of the Boy Bishop as a kind of crisis to be tided over with as little damage and scandal as might be, but the manner of Bishop Hallam was awakening the Dean to a sense of its original intention.

For Hallam was a man of deep devotion, and was keenly alive to the abuses of the Church of the fifteenth century, and anxious to revive the true spirit of piety. In the two years since he had come to Salisbury, much that was amiss had been amended in the diocese, and there had been much quickening of zeal and devotion, while proportionate discontent and anger had been excited in those who hated interference with their ease, their profits, their vices, or their superstitions.

Among the improvements he had introduced, was the much greater attention paid to the children of the choir. Till his time they had been drilled and flogged into performing their parts in the service, but with utter indifference whether they understood the words which their voices chanted, and likewise to their conduct, both in and out of Church. The same lad who would be beaten savagely for a false note, might tell falsehoods, steal apples, and devour them in the Cathedral with impunity so far as the authorities were concerned. Now, however, the boys were carefully schooled under the care of a clerk appointed by the Precentor, who was deservedly viewed as a gentle master, in spite of his profuse employment of the rod, the only means of discipline. However, he heartily loved his boys, and most of them loved him, though none so well as little Oswald of Amesbury, the very flower of the choir for his fair face, sweet voice, and gentle reverence, though his wit was perhaps less keen and bright than some of the others.

Slow he was in learning to read either manuscript or prick song, and still slower in comprehension of the Latinity which the boys were taught. At least, each of the others could more quickly translate a word, or conjugate a verb, and yet he could chant Psalms for ever, and there were looks and tones that made his master sure that he entered into the meaning, even though he could not explain it.

At the summons, the choir boys trooped into the beautiful Chapter-house, and stood round the tall central column of Purbeck marble supporting the groined roof. Their eyes did not as usual rest on the quaint figures in which the Scripture history is portrayed round the walls, but were eagerly fixed on the Bishop, who with the Dean, and others of the clergy round him, stood beneath the pillar. The foremost boy, dark-eyed and haired, with heavy brows, was Richard, or Diccon, the son of the Fletcher, or arrow-maker. He stood forth with a confident and eager air, while the others hung back a little, and among their brown heads could be seen the bright, light flaxen locks of the little shepherd of Stonehenge.

'Children,' asked the Bishop, 'do ye understand wherefore I have called you hither?'

'To choose our Bishop!' said Diccon (he had very nearly said to choose me).

'Know you wherefore the Procession of the Boy Bishop was instituted?' further demanded the Bishop.

'To make sport, and get alms,' replied Diccon without hesitation.

'Can none of you render me any other reason?' asked the Bishop.

No one spoke, but Oswald looked up with an eagerness in his eyes, as if he knew something, but could not utter it.

Then Bishop Robert told the boys in words they could understand, how the Holy Innocents had been the first to glorify the Saviour in His infancy by their martyrdom, and how they were now sharing His victory and triumph in Heaven; and how it had been planned by good men of old that the little children trained to sing the praise of God on earth, should, on the day of the Innocents, set forth before men's eyes some slight sign and token of how these children and the like pure and holy souls, redeemed out of this sinful world, while yet their baptismal dew was undried, and they were untainted by sin, follow the Lamb in Heaven, and sing the song that none other can learn. The boys all listened with bent heads, some with thoughtful faces; and Oswald's eyes were moist. No one spoke. 'None can be worthy enough, you are thinking, my children, to represent thus on earth the holy ones in Heaven. It is sooth, only too sooth. But we must do our best by God's grace to cleanse ourselves, body and soul, to set forth His praise and honour. Now speak, my dear children, and say which of you ye think most true and pure, and most meet to be your leader in this solemn work of praise.'

There was a pause; the boys were unwilling to speak, and the Precentor again put the question—

'Speak, lads; tell my Lord whom you think the best and meetest to lead you in the holy work on Childermas Day. What sayest thou, Harry of the Forge? Fear not. Say on.'

Harry, an open-faced boy, was the first to say—

'Little Oswald is the best lad of us.'

And then, one after another made the same reply—

'Little Oswald is meetest.'

Only three had not yet spoken—Oswald, Diccon, and a timid, shy boy, who always seemed trying to hide himself. When the question was put to the last, he faltered out—

'Diccon, sir.'

And Diccon himself looked up with bold, unabashed brow, and said—

'I'm oldest here, sir.'

'Thou mayst be oldest,' said the Bishop, 'but that is not what we are bidden to think of. The matter in hand is to take him who will most heartily and truly strive to praise God, and lead men to think of the choirs of the saints before His throne. My son, is that what thou dost think of in desiring this preferment?'

'As much as another,' muttered Diccon, as sulkily as he durst.

But out of the four-and-twenty lads there had been twenty-one voices declaring little Oswald the best. There was no doubt about his election. He had indeed replied 'Harry,' when asked for his vote, and when the Bishop laid his hand on him, and declared him elected as *Episcopus Puerorum*, he looked dazed and bewildered.

Some of the chapter observed to one another—

'Fair as an Angel indeed, but a mere puppet.'

And Diccon went away muttering that his father would see him righted, or know the reason why.

CHAPTER III.

WHOEVER devised the ritual of the Boy Bishop must have been
>Trying to wind himself too high
>For sinful men beneath the sky.

Beautiful as was the idea, and exquisite as the service was, it could scarce be carried out consistently by any human creatures on earth; and, in the Middle Ages, in a tongue not 'understood of the people,' and left to rude provincial ecclesiastics amid a ruder mob, the ceremony had degenerated into a popular holiday when sacrilegious profanity was in a manner licensed.

It was on St. Nicolas' day, the 6th of December, that the election took place, and the little Bishop continued in office till Innocents' day, the 28th. The early part of these three weeks was spent in training and singing, after which, when Mass was over on Christmas Day, the whole band of choristers went from house to house, in miniature ecclesiastical vestments, singing hymns and Christmas carols, and the two appointed deacons presenting bags, where alms were collected to maintain the lads if they continued to be educated for the priesthood. To prevent these customs from degenerating into idle roaming and shouting, the Dean had provided that the troop should be attended by trustworthy men, who kept order, and prevented them from being disturbed. It was fine frosty weather, and the boys went blithely forth, crackling through the ice-bound meadows, or climbing the downs, ever getting fresh views of the majestic spire, then only recently finished, and completing the wondrous grace of the whole building, which, in its freshness and unity yet variety, of peak, roof, and pinnacle, seemed like some magnificent iceberg rising in the midst of its valley.

Little Oswald was very happy that first morning. What he would have liked would have been to have gone to Amesbury, and to have sung before the kind nuns there, who would have rejoiced to see him in such array. The master, however, decided that this would be too far on these short days, and scarcely safe; for Salisbury Plain was not free from robbers, under the disturbed reign of Henry IV., and they might not even respect a Boy Bishop's bag of alms. However, Oswald was consoled by hearing that notice of his promotion had been sent, and that it was not impossible that his dear Lady Prioress might be present at the Cathedral itself on Childermas Day.

The only drawback was the surly manner and continual petty taunts and vexations he suffered from Diccon Fletcher. The lad had been, by way of consolation, made one of the attendant deacons, who had their share both of finery and of money; but this gave him the opportunity of venting his spite in many a 'nip and bob,' sly pushes, threats, and attempts to put him out in his singing, and what Oswald hated far more, introducing idle parodies on the sacred words, which long had been part of the traditional grotesqueness attached to the ceremony in the popular mind. These set the other boys—even Harry—giggling, and disposed Oswald to cry, while their master never was able to detect them, and the whole choir were too much afraid of Diccon to betray him. The master only saw that as the day went on the boys were harder to manage, and that the little Bishop's head drooped under his small mitre, and he was glad to bring them home after they had rested and been regaled with wassail bread and spiced ale, and presented with a comfit apiece by the kind admiring nuns of the Abbey at Wilton.

Their next day's rounds were in the city of Salisbury itself, where they sang in each of the chief houses of the nobles and gentry, who were apt to come into the city for the winter, and likewise in the streets and courts where the shops consisted of open stalls or booths, with the wares arranged in front, or hanging from the beams of the floor above. Thus it was they came to the stall of Denis the Fletcher, father to Diccon, where long yew bows and cloth-yard shafts in quivers, or arranged in a *chevaux de frise*, were the chief decoration.

Friar Piers, a red-faced, bronzed man, about thirty, in a Franciscan's gown and hood, was sitting at his ease in the corner of the stall, and joined the carol in a loud, lusty voice, unblushingly using the worst form of parody. When the song was over, he broke into a loud laugh, and on some remonstrance from the master, answered—

'What, sir clerk, I'm no slave to your Bishop. He can't mar the jolly friar's sport, do what he will to these poor boys. Times are changed since I lifted up my voice in the choir.'

'Aye, aye,' said his father, a big, brawny man, leaning over the window, 'then 'twas worth one's while to be Boy Bishop. Now I wouldn't give a tuft of goose down for it, nor Diccon either—only bedizening and psalm-singing, like mean beggarly Lollards. But come in, my lads, come in, and we'll show you some sport for once.'

The master here interfered, and said the Dean's and Precentor's orders were precise that the boys should enter no houses.

Friar Piers on this laughed, and said—

'They mistook the season, Master. Dost think they are creeping to the cross? It's merry Christmas, man, not Lent.'

'There! there's gospel for it. Hear the reverend brother,' cried Denis. 'Come in, boys—come in, gossips; there's a brimming cup of hot ale for you this cold day, better than any your Dean e'er gave you.'

The master still refused, but half the boys had been already led in by Diccon, and some of the escort were not proof against the good ale and good fellowship, and entered after the boys.

The master hardly knew what to do, whether to follow them in and try to bring them away, or to take home such as he could detain. While he was still in the gathering twilight, calling and entreating, Oswald suddenly felt a heavy hand on his shoulder.

'I don't want to come in,' he tried to say, a good deal frightened; but he was dragged along, with a hand over his mouth, into a dark entry beside the shop, and heard Denis's rough voice in his ear—

'Stand still, thou nuns' mammet, a plague on thee, or it shall be the worse for thee. Hold thy tongue and hearken. Knowest thou what thou deservest for thrusting thyself into the office that belonged of right to my Dick?'

'Oh, sir, 'twas none of my seeking. Let me go.'

'Whisht! I say, I grudge thee not thy fool's cap and sorry sport, so long as thou makest up for it in weightier matters. Listen! Sir Edward Fleming, the Canon, is dead. Thou must get thee back to thy Bishop and Dean, stand before them, and speak thus: " I, *Episcopus Puerorum Puerarum*, or however the gibberish runs, do appoint the Brother Piers Fletcher, of the Friars' Minorite, to the vacant canonry." Dost hear?'

'Yes, sir; but, sir,' said Oswald with a trembling voice, 'I am told that the Bishop and my master would not have it so.'

'What of that? Willy, nilly, if thou sayest it it must be done. None can gainsay the appointments of the Bairn Bishop. Now, mark me. If thou dost this at my bidding, I'll overlook the wrong that was done in thy foolish person to my son Richard. If not, thou shalt never live to rue the day! Not a word to any man, remember, that I have thus spoken. If thou dost, 'tis at thy peril. But if those words, appointing Piers Fletcher to the canonry, be not spoken, ere thy mummeries to-morrow be over, thou wilt never see another morn. There! Denis Fletcher is a man of his word!'

Wherewith Oswald, with his mitre knocked over his eyes, was pushed out into the street again, just as the master, with Harry and two or three of the steadier boys and men, came forth through the shop. The schoolmaster, believing that Diccon's family were most likely to vent their jealous spite on the little fellow, and unwilling to involve the choir in a quarrel with the townspeople at such a critical moment, asked no questions, but contented himself with returning to the monastery with the pupils he had been able to bring off, and winked at the disorderly manner in which the others straggled in later.

No one but Harry saw that the little Boy Bishop looked pale and dazed in the light of the big fire on the hearth of the refectory, and that he scarce touched food, and passed the horn of Christmas ale that was handed round. Moreover, when in the dormitory, Harry had fallen asleep, and wakened again to hear Diccon, who had come in much later, thus threatening the child—

'What, mumbling thy prayers still, thou beggars' brat! None of that, I say. Bishop or no Bishop, I'm master here. Into bed, I say.'

And a sounding box on the ear was heard. On this Harry started out of bed with a yell of wrath, and fell on the tyrant; but therewith a torch shone on them, and the master was heard calling fie on them for such a brawl, and threatening Diccon and Harry alike with stripes if another sound were heard. Good-natured Harry tumbled into bed, and tried to warm and comfort the shivering, sobbing little being who clung to him; but it was not then possible to speak, and Harry slept, and woke again, with the moonlight streaming through the chinks of the rude wooden shutter of the unglazed window, and the snores of the other boys around. He knew, however, that his bed-fellow was awake, and he ventured a whisper—

'Tell me, Oswald, what is it? Did that felon misuse thee?'

'Nay,' said Oswald.

'What then? Did he scare thee out of thy five wits that thou prayedst so long?'

'Aye,' said Oswald. But he said no more, only as Harry muttered some sharp and angry words the child trembled again, and prayed him to be still, and utter no word to anyone.

Harry was very sleepy, and gave the promise, then fell asleep. In aftertimes he greatly longed to have been more alive to the child's distress, and to have guessed what troubled him; but Oswald was at times dreamy, and always had little power of expressing himself, so that no one could have guessed whether he understood what Denis required of him, or entered into the threat, or whether he were merely frightened and bewildered.

Morning dawned at last. The choir boys were

not whipped out of bed like their fellows in the city, but they were arrayed, not in the less costly garb in which they had gone about singing, but in the full vestments made for their use.

Oswald was, on first waking, handed over to the brother who had charge of the robes. He was bathed, and his fair hair carefully arranged, after which he was arrayed in a robe of scarlet worked with silver lions and a border of gold birds: over this came the alb starred over with gold, and above a white cope richly bordered with embroidery in red silk and gold. A ring with a large sapphire in it was placed on his finger, and on his head a mitre 'well garnished with pearl and precious stone.' A book—the Pontificate, richly bound, with a blue stone set on its cover, was to be carried in one hand, and a small processional cross, adorned with the figure of St. Nicolas, was to be borne before him by one of the boys. Another carried a banner of St. Nicolas, and all were richly arrayed, the two deacons in scarlet above and blue beneath. Oswald seemed to have slept off his fright, and to be pleased with his splendid dress, though still somewhat as if in a dream, for he asked—

'Be these like the robes the Innocents wear? Methought they had made them white.'

The great west door of the Cathedral was thrown open, and up the broad aisle, beneath the graceful pointed arches, beneath the tall-clustered columns, came the goodly procession. The Dean and his chapter going first, in gorgeous array—then the banner of St. Nicolas and a little cross; then the chorister children in their rich array, two-and-two, each with a lighted taper in his hand; the little Bishop, a quaint but yet a lovely figure, walking, attended by his two deacons, chanting the words, *Centum quatuor quadraginta signati sunt.* They were the familiar words of Revelation vii. 'A hundred and forty and four thousand were sealed.' Up the long nave went the procession, beautiful as a miniature; the clear, sweet voice of little Bishop Oswald beginning each verse, *Ex tribu Juda; ex tribu Reuben*; and the deacons, and the full body of the choristers taking up the chorus, *Duodecim millia signati.*

The loveliness of the sight and sound was unspeakable, while the gleam of the tapers vied with the wintry sunshine, in the south-east, in casting strange glances from their gold and jewels upon the roof. There was something unearthly in the whole scene, above all when, at the Altar of the Holy Innocents, the chant changed to our actual Innocents'-day epistle, 'I looked,' &c. Three voices then sung *Illi sunt emti* ('These are redeemed from among men, being the firstfruits unto God and unto the Lamb. And in their mouth was found no guile, for they are without fault before the throne of God.')

Meantime with a censer in his hand, the Chorister Bishop fumed the Altar, and then said (in Latin), 'Let us be glad,' to which the answer was, 'And let us rejoice.'

The little one's face was rapt and beautiful to behold, as he stood swinging his censer, and therewith he knelt and uttered in Latin the collect we know so well for that day, though our translation is slightly altered at the opening, which then was: 'Almighty God, Whose fame on this day the innocent martyrs confessed not by speech but by death. Mortify and kill all vices in us, and so strengthen us by Thy Grace, that by our tongue we may speak, and by our life we may set forth, the glory of Thy Holy Name, Who with the Father and Holy Ghost art ever worshipped and glorified.—Amen.

Then the procession entered the Choir, being now joined by the clergy of the Cathedral, the Dean and his canons going first, and taking the places around the Altar; and then the children's procession coming last, with the little Bishop and his small chapter at the end, so that he was seated in the place of honour on one side of the gate into the choir, and his chief deacon on the opposite side, preparatory to high Mass being celebrated by the real Bishop.

No one took note when Diccon Fletcher, as they were ranging themselves, grasped Oswald's shoulder, and whispered in his ear—

'Remember, now's the time. Speak when thou get to thy seat.'

Nor was the surging and shouting of a multitude without, at first heard through the singing, and the orderly tread of feet. The stalls were reached, and ere Diccon turned into his own, he gave the Bishop another grip, and said—

'Now! out with it—*I, Episcopus Puerorum.* Speak, or it will be the worse for thee.'

Here a minor canon, seeing that there was whispering among the boys, summarily showed Diccon into his place, and the Child Bishop took his seat, looking a little pale under his mitre.

At that moment the surging sound came nearer. The comparatively well-behaved throng, who had hitherto filled the nave, save where the gangway was kept free for the procession, was pushed hither and thither. The sacristan and his fellows, who had been keeping order, were driven in from the doors, and up the aisles rushed tumultuously a rush of merrymakers, some with cocks' combs, some with caps and bells, fools' coats, birds' beaks, asses' heads, stags' or bullocks' horns, all manner of carnival foolery, making the nave, where the children's chant had so lately resounded, echo to foul and ludicrous songs set to sacred tunes.

No one was so near the choir gates as Oswald on the one side, Diccon on the other. Each started forward, the one to close them, the other to prevent him from doing so, and therewith the elder boy caught the younger in a tight clutch, saying—

'Speak.'

At the same moment a black-masked and horned figure sprang forth, and laid a black hand and arm on the child's shoulder.

'Face about,' he said. 'Say the words and I let thee go!'

The eyes stared as if fixed, lips quivered, recurring as it were to their recent lesson, *Laudamini et Gloriamini.* Priests and canons rallying from their amazement, were coming to the rescue; but at that moment the demoniacal form seemed to vanish, while the Boy Bishop, released from his grasp with violence, fell headlong down the step between the nave and choir, and lay motionless at the bottom. There was one shriek from one of the boys. Then came the stillness of horror. Then the master of the choristers was kneeling beside the little prostrate figure, lifting him up. His cross-bearer had rushed to his side, and at the same moment the black-veiled and hooded

Prioress broke from her seat in the choir, and Bishop Robert hurried from the Altar.

'Oswald, dear child, look up,' said the Prioress, taking a feeble, nerveless hand in hers, as the master drew off the mitre. At her voice, as regardless of rule in that moment, she threw back her veil, the blue eyes unclosed, the lips seemed to continue their lesson, and the words came forth, '*Non loquendo sed moriendo.*' There was an instant's struggle, then the fair head fell back, and Hallam looked up and, with uplifted hand, said to the people, '*Non loquendo sed moriendo.* Not by speech, but death, the innocent hath glorified God, by dying in hindering your profane and heedless folly. Go home, you who know not what ye did. Go home, and repent of your folly and madness, if perchance, it may be forgiven.'

Then—as the dismayed multitudes, many of the women weeping and sobbing—began to drift away, remembering with dread the heavy anathemas that those incurred who should interfere with the procession of the children, the Bishop turned again to the Prioress who was weeping soft tears as she knelt beside the dead child.

'Good Mother,' he said, 'thou hast cause to rejoice. Thy nursling hath truly followed the Lamb in life and death. Now will he indeed follow Him whithersoever He goeth, having gone with the dew of Grace still fresh on his brow.'

The Prioress looked up through her natural tears of pity, and soon was comforted, to think of the sweet child who had been her nuns' plaything, being thus delivered from the heavy trials of this rude and troublesome world, but the Bishop took—as he said—grief and repentance to himself for having endeavoured to carry out an ordinance fit indeed, as Holy Writ showed, only for the very highest and holiest saints in Heaven, among those who could not by any means represent it rightly or without profane imitation at the best.

There was a mark of a blow on the child's temple, but whether given by hand or received in the fall, no one could tell. For three days Oswald lay in state before the Altar of the Holy Innocents, his childish face full of unearthly beauty. Then he was buried amid the tears of all Salisbury, and his effigy in his robes was set up over his tomb, and it is still within the Cathedral, though it has been moved from his actual grave, and now lies between two of the pillars of the nave.

There was no attempt to trace who was the masker who had attacked him. He was beyond the reach of the laws of the country, since the child was reckoned as a clerk. Nor indeed did anyone guess that more had been at stake than the protection of the choir from the intrusion of the mob. More than a year after, however, Bishop Hallam was sought out by a miserable, broken-hearted man, Denis the Fletcher. Diccon had run away from home in disgrace; Piers had been caught in a drunken brawl, and was under restraint by the Prior of his order; he himself had lost his trade and had nearly come to beggary, and convinced that all was the effect of the curses his sin had incurred, he came to pour out all to the Bishop. He had not intended murder, but had been driven into blind passion by being thwarted by the passive resistance which to him appeared stupid obstinacy.

And what was it? Had Oswald really known what he was doing? Had he embraced death rather than promote an unworthy man? Could the young and simple little shepherd have understood the grave issues of the matter? Or had he been merely too timid and awestruck, and too dull to understand what was required of him? Or, what might be more likely, did he faithfully act on a sound instinct that to do the bidding of a man like Denis would be disobedience to those whom he was bound to obey?

None could say, not even Harry, who had known the child best, and who was growing up to be a youth of much promise. All that could be known was that Oswald, the Boy Bishop, had gone to join the Innocents in the midst of defending the honour of his God, whether consciously or unconsciously.

Seven years later the Cardinal Bishop, Robert Hallam, lay dying in the chamber of an over-crowded hostel at Constance. He was spent with months of effort to reform the abuses of the Church (among them this very festival of the Boy Bishop), and to make her clergy into real shepherds instead of hirelings, so that profaneness and violence might not so often defile the holiest things. And now he was dying, worn out by the conflict, baffled, and, as some deemed, poisoned by the men who 'hated to be reformed, and had cast God's words behind them.'

'Ah, well,' he said, to his sorrowing chaplain, 'there are times when all that is left for a man to do, is to die like little Oswald in guarding the sanctuary gates. *Non loquendo sed moriendo*, said he. I have spoken. Since they will not hear, I can only die, trusting that the Dew of His Grace will never be dried up from His Church.'

Darker days did indeed follow on his death, but in the shortly ensuing Council of Basle, the festival of the Boy Bishop was abolished; and thwarted, and turned aside, as it has often been, the quickening Dew has never been wanting. Even in the darkest, driest ages, some green spots have testified to that refreshing grace ; and ever and anon, vigour and energy improving and shaking off old evil, prove that still that Spirit Who 'maketh all things new' is poured upon the Church.

ONE WILL AND THREE WAYS.

Where there's a will there's a **way.**

CHAPTER I.

THE THREE MAIDENS.

THREE maidens were crouching together on one large bed, with a high carved oaken back and canopy, and heavy tapestry curtains. They were linked tightly in one another's arms, as if clinging together lessened their sense of desolation, and when one or other broke into sobs and wailing, the others kissed and cheered, and soothed her as best they might.

Their castle, by name the Tower of the Mere, from its situation on a small remote lake in the heart of the Cumberland mountains, had that afternoon received the Earl of Pembroke's pursuivant on his way from Scotland, and through him they had learnt the tidings that their father, Sir Thomas d'Estouteville, commonly called Stout Tom of the Meres, had been made prisoner in a skirmish with Sir Edward de Bruce.

Gilbert Dutton, the grey-haired pursuivant, scrupled not to declare that a charge of twenty men-at-arms would have saved the knight; but the King had forbidden this lest it should bring on a battle, and fiercely had my Lord of Pembroke chafed at himself for having waited for orders, and still more at the deadly blight which had come over the manhood of England, when the 'Hammer of the Scots' had breathed his last at Burgh-on-the-Sands.

The earl, an old friend and patron of Sir Thomas, had sent Dutton to bear the tidings to the Tower, and tell the daughters that their father's ransom had been fixed at 15,000 crowns, which they ought to regard as the greatest possible compliment to his valour. The pursuivant was on his way to London, but he would visit the Tower again in returning to Scotland, in case they had any greetings to send Sir Thomas, or an instalment of his ransom.

The eldest sister, Ankaret, had thanked him, and inquired the time of his return, with so much composure and dignity, that the younger ones, Blanche and little Gillian, never doubted that she knew where to lay her hands on the sum required. Ankaret was five years older than the next sister, and looked much more. She was pale and worn, and halted a little in her gait, having never quite recovered a bad fall on her way home from the convent at Whitby. Her accident had deferred her wedding with young Nigel Bruce, whose brother was at that time a Cumbrian, as well as a Scottish, noble and an obedient vassal of Edward I.

Before she had quitted her sick bed, the Bruces were at the head of the national party in Scotland, and the next winter, Nigel was taken in Kildrummie Castle, and suffered a traitor's death. From thenceforth, Ankaret had looked on the cloister as her destination and refuge; but her mother's death threw the whole household care upon her, together with the charge of her little sister Gillian. Her countenance, bearing the tokens of peace won after a great storm of sorrow, her still calm voice and demeanour, and her avowed dedication to a religious life, made her be regarded as a sufficient authority in the family, where she maintained excellent order and discipline; while she was devotedly loved by all who came under her influence.

Blanche, who was just sixteen, had been brought home a few months previously from a small country priory not far off, to be inspected by a baron, who wanted an Estouteville heiress for his son, but finding her portion less than he had expected, had withdrawn from the contract. However, as the parties had never met, this had not much hurt her spirits. Little Gillian had never left home. Her father could not make up his mind to part with her, and she had climbed the mountains, ridden her rough pony, hunted and hawked, and delighted to be called his bonnie lad, trying to forget that she was but a lass. She was eleven years old, and her sister was supposed to teach her all convent arts of stitchery and confections; but she was the least amenable of all Ankaret's subjects; she tore more garments than she sewed, and could gather and eat whortleberries much better than preserve them with honey. However, since her chief playfellow, her father, had been in Scotland, her sisters had made her spin a little, but very 'silly' was the thread, and often was the spinster missed, and found careering round the court with the dogs, paddling in the mere, or climbing the craig to call home the goats.

But now little Gillian's merry eyes were swollen with such tears as she had never shed before, for Ankaret had declared that all the coin in the casket had been spent on arms for the men who had gone to Scotland with Sir Thomas. It was the remnant of the ransom of his last captives. Rents there were none; dues were paid in kind or by labour; and ready money was not to be had! What could be done? To pledge the castle and lands to some rich monastery, or to the Bishop, had been Ankaret's first thought, and she had held counsel with the chaplain about it; but he had told her that the worth of the whole of the little mountain nook was not a third of the ransom, and that, moreover, all the Church property had been so much harried of late by the Scots, and so much had been called for by the King's extravagances, that she must not hope to borrow from prelate, abbot, nor Lombard.

The King could never let a brave warrior waste in a dungeon. He would set him free. So said little Gillian; but her sisters knew too well that King Edward had rather deck Piers Gaveston in gold and jewels than spare a mark to deliver a brave man from captivity; and they wept again for the good and great King Edward, whose death-bed at Burgh-on-the-Sands their father had attended.

At last, little Gillian, worn out with tears, fell asleep in Ankaret's arms; the others kept still in order not to disturb her, and Blanche soon slumbered too; but Ankaret, though motionless and dry-eyed, lay long, with a terrible ache at her heart, that the harshness of such an excessive ransom should have come from the Bruces, of all others. Could they not have dealt kindly with her father for Nigel's sake, instead of dooming him to what they must know would be, to a man of his means, endless captivity?

She lay, while the moonlight passed from the south loophole to the western, and then was lost in the morning light. The other two may have awakened, but none moved till the morning stir began, and then Gillian started to her feet, crying, 'I know what I will do. Father shall not be left in prison!'

Blanche sat up, and parting back her hair with her hands, looked resolute, and said, 'I have my plan. Father shall not be left in prison!'

Ankaret crossed their brows with drops from the holy-water stoup, and said—'If it be God's will—Father shall not be left in prison!'

'I shall go to him, and file his fetters through,' cried Gillian, her dark eyes glittering. Her sisters smiled at her confident proposal, and she cried, 'Yea, it was the mouse that freed the lion in the barefoot Friar's sermon! Father is the lion, and his little Jill is the mouse.'

'Well spoken, mighty mouse,' said Blanche, eager to tell her own scheme. 'Ankaret, I will to the Court, when high festival is holden, and will pray King Edward to grant me a champion. I will offer myself and all that I have to the good knight and true who shall deliver my father. If there be knighthood in England, or power in a fair face, he shall be freed!' And Blanche swept back her profuse flaxen tresses, showing a face between so white-skinned and rose-tinted, with such lovely features, that her fond elder sister thought no true knight or squire could hold back from such a suppliant's request.

'But how canst thou reach the Court?' she asked.

'I'll find the way. My noble godfather—my Lord of Pembroke will aid me.'

'And what wilt thou do for father, sister?' said the little one, turning to Ankaret, almost as if it were a game.

'I can but aid with my prayers,' said she. 'Add my third of our heritage to thine, Blanche, if that will serve to win thee a champion. Lands may profit thee, and they are not needed by a poor bedeswoman.'

CHAPTER II.

THE MOUSE.

Spring was making the bonnie north countrie green and beautiful. The mountains rose like purple clouds, with fantastic masses of white in their hollows, the torrents rushed headlong down their clefts, to dance and babble in the clear streams below, the grass grew rich and lush, the trees were white with blossom, the flowers carpeted every bank, the bushes rang with the notes of the blackbird and thrush, the lakes reflected the clear brilliancy of the sky and the rich colouring of the mountains.

Young Maurice Dutton thought he had never seen a fairer spot, as his heart leapt within him, and he longed for a gallop on the green sward that bordered lovely Ulswater. He was the pursuivant's grandson, a lad of fifteen, making his first outset in the train of his grandsire. The previous day had been spent at the Tower of the Mere, which, according to promise, Gilbert Dutton had visited on his return to carry a message from Pembroke to the Scottish enemy. He had received from the young ladies for their father's behoof, a purse, a letter, and a bundle of raiment, and Gillian's coaxing entreaties had also prevailed with him to take with him the knight's favourite hound as a solace to his captivity. Maurice had undertaken the charge, but he was beginning to rue the attention he had paid to the little maiden's blandishments, for Lenoir would by no means consent to be dragged away from home, and tugged at the leash so as nearly to pull him off his horse, and the men-at-arms who were riding near advised that the beast should be let go, while he could still find his way back.

Suddenly Lenoir made a bound, which broke the leash, and began with frantic barks to dance round a young boy on a rough pony who was alongside of them.

'Hallo, there!' called Maurice; 'dost know the dog?'

'Aye, sir,' was the answer, in a clear young voice; 'he will follow me without the leash.'

'Thou are not going with us?'

'Yes, I am, sir; I have a charge.'

'What from the ladies of the Mere?'

'From Sir Thomas d'Estouteville's daughters. I could not set off with you, but I followed.'

'I knew nought of this. Didst thou, Will?' asked young Dutton.

'Not I, sir. Belike the ladies settled it with the pursuivant.'

Maurice came to the same conclusion; but he could not consult his grandfather, for the priest of Keswick, delighted to fall in with anyone fresh from court, was riding with the party conversing. The pursuivant himself, a man of peace, had only four attendants, but they were accompanied by twenty men-at-arms, on the way to reinforce one of Lord Pembroke's Scottish garrisons. No sooner did the captain observe the boy than he called out, 'Hallo! what have we here?'

Maurice made answer, ''Tis a page whom Sir Thomas d'Estouteville's daughters are sending him.'

'A page! Another mammet to dandle,' laughed the captain. 'How now, youngster, what's thy name?'

'Giles, at your service,' and the boy turned on his saddle to face the inquirer with a sort of frightened audacity. He was a pretty fellow, with a brightly tinted, somewhat weather-browned face, quick dark eyes, and hair roughly trimmed under a little crimson cap, to which a black cock's double-curved tail gave a jaunty air, and he was dressed in a grey homespun suit. His expression was saucy and yet half scared, and some of the soldiers would have baited him with rough jokes, but that Maurice first answered for him, and then kept him out of their way.

Old Gilbert Dutton himself may have thought the child belonged to the soldiers, for he never noticed him during the mid-day rest. In the evening there was a halt at a peel tower on the Solway, held by an English knight. Here the grandfather, anxious to practise Maurice in the duties of a page, kept him employed at the supper table, so that he could not snatch his own meal till the knight and squire had finished; and the former was listening to the oft-told tale of Gaveston's insults to the nobles, how he called their own Lord Pembroke himself, Joseph the Jew, the Earl of Warwick, the black dog of Ardennes, and the Earl of Lancaster, the stage-player; also how the king demeaned himself by going about in a barge on the Thames chaffering for cabbages like any costermonger. Amid the growls of vexation and censure, and the whispers that measures must be taken against the arrogant minion, Maurice looked about for the small Giles, and finding him nowhere in the hall, betook himself to the lower story of the tower, which was used as stable, byre, pigstye, henroost, and likewise bedroom for all not of exalted rank.

The human inhabitants were at supper in the hall above, and though there it was still daylight, darkness was fast coming over this vaulted almost unlighted place, as Maurice descended the stone stair hearing all around the rattling of chains, the champing of horses' teeth, and the hollow tramp of their hoofs, but through all he distinguished a little sobbing. Directed by which he found his way to where the rough pony stood. There, with arms around Lenoir, sitting up, startled, and trying to choke down the sobs as a step approached, was their volunteer comrade.

'Ho, Mistress Gillian!' was Maurice's address. 'Art ready to go back again?'

'Gillian me no Gillians,' was the answer, with a passionate leap on her feet. 'Thou art a malapert lad to spy me out and flout me.'

Amazed at the ready wit which repelled his greeting as the mere twitting a boy with girlish tears, Maurice added in his teasing voice, 'There was more of Gillian than of Giles in thy courtesy when Sir John met us.'

'Oh, Maurice,' she said, abandoning her disguise, 'thou wilt not tell. Did anyone see it but thou?'

'I thought thou wast crying to get home to thy sisters.'

'No, indeed! I'm going to deliver my father!'

'A fine deliverer, sobbing in the straw!'

'I shall never do that again.'

'For thou wilt be at home to-morrow night.'

'Thou hast not told?' she cried, passionately. Perhaps he would have tormented her longer had not ringing steps on the stairs warned them that they should not be alone much longer, so they dropped down together in the straw by the pony's nose while Gillian pleaded. 'If thou hadst a father in prison, wouldst thou not go to him?'

'I'm not a wench. I could do some good.'

'But father has no son. I always was his boy. I I must go; and see—I've got the armourer's file, and shall break his chain for him. Good Maurice Dutton, remember the whortleberries and cream I gave thee, and betray me not! And I will give you Sweetheart's blackest pup and love you for evermore.'

Maurice had a soft heart, and admired her spirit, while, boylike, he enjoyed outwitting his elders; and he let her eloquence prevail, but with many warnings not to betray herself, as his grandfather would be sure to think smuggling her in, not consistent with the honour of the heraldic profession, of which he was very jealous. At present, he thought she belonged to the soldiers, as they thought she belonged to him, but if he discovered who she was, she would certainly be sent home. Her tears had sprung from loneliness and the first experience of neglect and longing for her sisters and home; but when she had Maurice to speak to, her spirit revived, and she was happy again. She did not mind roughing it; and was pretty well inured to hardships in hunting excursions with her father;

the mode of riding was no novelty to her, so that among a party who cared not at all about a very small page, she attracted no observation, while Maurice was ever ready to shield, help, and protect her, letting no one tease her except himself.

When the pursuivant and the captain came to an understanding that the stranger belonged to neither of them, Maurice was applied to about him, and answered warily: 'He is from the Meres. He says his name is Giles, and that the ladies have sent him under your care to their father.'

Gilbert Dutton taxed his memory whether he had received such a request, knowing that he should not have granted it; but he was an old man, and had had a long ride, followed by a hearty meal of mountain kid and spiced Malvoisie, and he knew he had nodded, while Ankaret had been talking to him. In his uncertainty, he sent for 'Giles' and cross-examined him; but Gillian's readiness was a match for all questions, and he became so well convinced that his consent had been asked and given in his slumberous oblivion, as to make no further doubt about this member of his party.

In due time they reached Stirling, then the limit of Edward II.'s possessions. There the soldiers remained while the pursuivant went forward to Ayr, where Robert Bruce was recruiting his health at the baths, which are still, from his sojourn there, called

King's Ease, and where he founded an hospital for sufferers from the same disease as his own.

The whole country lay desolate with black patches and broken walls, marking where homesteads had once stood; and as the party went further west, it was over moorland and moss with scarce a sign of habitation till they approached the coast.

In a valley round the healing springs were a cluster of wooden houses and tents, and from a mound in the centre waved the Lion of Scotland. Here Maurice had told Gillian they should hear in what castle her father was imprisoned, and learn whether it was possible for her to reach him.

Dutton, in his heraldic surcoat of the blue and gold fesses of Valence, with the Fairy Melusina embroidered as the badge on his cap, was free to pass in with his suite, and was at once taken to the large barnlike erection which sheltered the national monarch and hero of Scotland. The great Robert was on a large carved chair, with his feet swathed and on a stool, by a smouldering peat fire in the centre of the room under a hole for the issue of the smoke. The walls were hung with pine branches, and decked with deer and wolf skins. Hooded hawks sat upon the antlers that projected from them, and dogs bayed at the entrance of the strangers.

But Gillian saw none of this. She only saw a

knight standing near King Robert, in the long robes of peace, not chained nor fettered, moving as freely as anyone present. She forgot that she was a boy, forgot that she was a humble little supernumerary page in the presence of a crowned king, forgot everything in that sight, and with a wild shriek of ecstasy, 'Father! father! father!' she flew past everyone, darted into his arms, and hid her face on his breast.

It was perhaps a fortunate interruption of the formalities, since no true Englishman could grant Bruce the title of the king, and he could listen to nothing addressed to him as Earl of Carrick. All Dutton could do was to show himself as much astounded as the rest; but he was hardly heeded. The king was watching the meeting with tears in his eyes, as he thought of his own Marjorie, his only child, a captive from her babyhood in England. Little Gillian was the heroine of the hour, and when her father led her to the king to ask his pardon, the royal warrior bent down and kissed her brow, telling her she was a leal wee lassie. She sat between him and her father at supper, and made them sport with her lively prattle on the incidents of her journey. But when her father took her to his own tent where she was to sleep, he was much graver, and asked her what Ankaret had said to her enterprise.

'Ankaret and Blanche treated it all as folly,' said she, pouting.

'And thou camest away unknown to them. Poor Ankaret, thou hast brought more trouble on her.'

'She *must* know where I am gone!'

'Great comfort in that! Alack! it is true that I have cockered thee over much, else wouldst thou never have dared this.'

'I came to set thee free. I have a file to break thy fetters, father. Why hast thou none?' she asked as if she were balked.

'Because a knight's word is stronger than iron, Gillian. I am a captive on parole to Sir Edward Bruce; and so, sweetheart, thy file is of no avail.'

The poor little mouse had found her lion under an impalpable net, against which her teeth were of no service. She hid her face and wept bitterly.

Moreover, all the ladies of the Scottish court being captive, her father knew not how to bestow her, save in a convent. He would not listen for a moment to her scheme of attending him in her page's trim. Dutton had to go to the Lord of Lorn in the north, and then return with all speed to his lord, so that he could not take her home, and all poor little Gillian gained by her attempt was incarceration in a solemn and strict Cistercian nunnery, among a number of little Scots, who called her a false Southron and thought more of her unfeminine freak, than of the filial devotion that had prompted it.

CHAPTER III.

THE VOW OF THE SWAN.

THE next October, King Edward kept his court at York, and there was high banquetting in the great hall where sat the king and queen, the two most beautiful people in England, crowned and gorgeously robed, surrounded by all that was young and splendid in the realm.

Blanche d'Estouteville thought nothing could rival the scene, as dazzled, flushed, and trembling, she waited behind a tall carved screen under the care of good old Gilbert Dutton. The Earl of Pembroke had at first undertaken to escort her himself; but on finding that Edward had recalled his unworthy favourite from Ireland, he had refused to attend the parliament of York, and had sent word to his god-daughter that she must wait for a more favourable opportunity. Blanche, however, would brook no delay. She thought the earl dull and lukewarm in his friend's cause, and believed that he was only making excuses. Sir Thomas had already been in prison a year, and he would die there unless she exerted herself at once, without waiting for slack friendship. Besides, York was the right place in which to look for the champion of a northern knight.

Lord Pembroke shrugged his shoulders at the folly and impatience of women, and foretold that she would make a bootless quest; but he permitted his old pursuivant to go and take care that the silly damsel came to no harm among the roistering gallants of the court. So while the maiden stood entranced by the magnificence of gold and jewels, feathers and robes, Dutton thought of the contrast with the court of a few years back, when noble, resolute men, grown grey in war and council, had sat in the seats now occupied by young fops with pointed hoods, witless; long coats, graceless. The Earl of Cornwall, as men, under severe penalties, were bidden to call Gaveston, a Gascon, with regular dark features, set off to the acmé of extravagant foppery, sat next to Queen Isabel, a brilliant blonde of sixteen, but with an expression of sullen discontent, while the king and his favourite laughed and talked across her, as if she were a mere child not worth attention. Edward himself had the perfect features of his race, and when at rest, there was something kingly and even pathetic in his face, but his laugh instantly betrayed his weakness and folly. Blanche, however, only beheld the splendour of his royalty, though it was more in his crown than his countenance. A king so fair must needs be kind. Did they say her father's cause would have been safe with stern old Longshanks? Far more must it prosper with so young and gracious a king. Music sounded in the gallery above. The Archbishop's choir and that of the Cathedral sang and made addresses; the first course had been eaten, and was being removed when Dutton touched the lady, and showed her Maurice and another page supporting between them an enormous silver dish on which was placed a stuffed swan, its neck arched, and its wings erected and crossed, after the graceful manner of its kind upon the water.

This was Blanche's signal. With her dark blue hood falling back and showing the long tresses of fair hair plaited with gold, that hung down on either side to her waist; and a rich blue robe, with long hanging gold embroidered sleeves, opening in front to show her white velvet skirt, she moved forward, closely followed by the pages carrying the swan, till, as she came in front of the king, she dropped on her knee on the step of the dais, and holding up her hands joined in supplication, exclaimed, 'A boon, a boon, my liege. I seek a knight who will deliver my father.'

There had been a moment's pause in the music

and revelry, in the expectation of a pageant, but long before Blanche had begun to speak, the buzz had begun again, and she could not hear what passed between the king and his immediate surroundings.

'Is't a device?'

'A mighty sorry one if it be.'

'That monster goose only comes forth as the shoeing horn to some wild goose chase.'

''Tis some insolence of the Stage player's.'

'Nay, I smell not Tom of Lancaster in this paltry device. Yonder is Aymar of Pembroke's old esquire bringing up the rear.'

'In sooth, the scantness of the trapping smacks of Joseph the Jew.'

'The wench is fair enough. We'll hear her.'

'Have a care, my lord. She has got by heart a speech three ells long, on the Scots' war, and the Commons' murmurs, and your poor Piers's misdeeds.'

'Never fear, gossip Piers. So soon as she runs into length, we bid pipe and cymbal strike up. Peace there! Can none of you keep your tongues still a moment?' Then turning to Blanche, who still knelt on the step, 'Speak, maiden; who sent thee here?'

'No man, my liege,' said Blanche, crimsoning, as she felt curious eyes scanning her. 'I came of my free will.'

'Out with it then,' said the king. 'On with the mumming.'

'I am no mummer, sir!' cried the girl, on her feet in an instant, her eyes sparkling with indignation. 'I am daughter to Sir Thomas d'Estouteville of the Meres, foully made captive in Scotland. I am here to crave your permission to offer my hand and portion to any good knight and true who will take up my cause, and obtain the freedom of my lord and father.'

She looked with eager passionate pleading along the rows of knights and dames, but she did not meet the return glance she expected. Some ladies were whispering, 'Her hood is in the fashion of the days of old Queen Eleanor!' Others, 'Brazen lass! thus to make a show of herself like a damosel in a Geste book;' while gentler dames sighed, that so fair and sweet-faced a maid should have no parents to guard and guide her.

Men muttered together a few criticisms on the beautiful imploring face, but chiefly questions on the worth of the Mere lands, and jokes upon the prize, as idle youth, in times of degeneracy, is ever wont to make game of what would have stirred their fathers to the very heart.

'Thou'dst best undertake it. The Tower will patch up thy debts.'

'Who—I? Dost think me such an oaf as to bury me alive in a grim Border castle? What sayest thou, Hugo? Thou hast a turn for castles and damosels. Here's a faite worthy of the docipairs themselves.'

'Did the docipairs ever undertake an emprise for a grim old father-in-law? Stout Tom would scarce give his daughter's husband seisin while he could hold a grip.'

'Dullard! As though his rescue might not be attempted in such sort as to make the Bruce tighten his grip, and maybe bestow him where he would trouble thee no more.'

This passed, while on the king signing consent, a horn was wound, and Dutton proclaimed—

'Oyez, oyez, oyez! Here standeth the noble damosel, Blanche d'Estouteville, of the Tower of the Mere, offering her fair hand and her inheritance of two-thirds of the Mere lands, to whomsoever of this company, being a knight, or esquire about to win his spurs, who will make the Vow of the Swan, to redeem from captivity, by ransom or exchange, her father, Sir Thomas d'Estouteville, the prisoner of the attainted traitor Sir Edward de Bruce.'

Three times the horn sounded, and Dutton made his proclamation. Blanche stood mute, with a crystal tear on each burning cheek. The second time a goodly youth would have sprung up, but was held down forcibly between his mother and elder brother, the one saying, 'No daring wench for my son's wife!' —the other—'Senseless lad, a mere bit of bare rock.' The youth was quenched, and the third proclamation followed. Blanche, with beating heart and tear-dimmed eye, was about to retreat, when there advanced a light slim figure, gaily clad in crimson, tawny, and blue robes, which made a brave appearance at first sight, though they were perhaps a little frayed and greasy. He had a brown face, dark, small glittering eyes, black hair, and moustache, and he bowed to the very floor, as he exclaimed, in a French accent, 'Never be it said that fair damsel craved succour in vain before Ferrand de Honifort. Madame, I offer myself, my sword, my horse, my purse, and an arm not unknown to fame, to deliver the doughty and renowned Sir Thomas d'Estouteville, deeming myself amply repaid by permission to kiss but once that fair hand.'

Dutton made a step forward, but held back, as Blanche, with a beaming look of joy, held out her hand, and he kissing it, and holding the tips of her fingers, asked the king's permission to undertake the feat of arms.

'Certes,' replied Edward. 'Thou art free to make thy fortune—if yonder goose will lay thee golden eggs,' he muttered aside.

Sir Ferrand de Honifort laid his hand on the Swan, and swore by it, to become the champion of the Lady Blanche, and win her father's freedom. There was a great outburst of applause, and the king called out, 'Well said, my Ferrand. To-morrow we'll see thy bridal to the Lady of the Swan. Ha, maiden, what sayest thou?'

'If he will deliver my father,' she faltered.

'Dost doubt me, lady?' cried Honifort. 'It ill beseems a man's tongue to speak of his own deeds, but Gascony, Navarre, Castille, France, Wales, Ireland, yea, and Scotland, can testify to the deeds of Ferrand de Honifort!'

Therewith he led her to a seat at the banquet table, and there, while fresh 'subtilties' and devices came in, and music brayed louder, she listened with wondering and delighted ear to stories of six Welshmen at once impaled on Honifort's lance; of Irish kernes slaughtered like sheep; of Poitevin castles won by escalade; and though she had imagined that her champion would be English, not Gascon, and likewise a good deal younger, she was completely won over, and quite believed that her Paladin would, as he promised, broil the Black Douglas in his own larder, and overthrow every castle in Scotland, to bring home Sir Thomas.

So she treated with scorn Dutton's entreaties at least to submit her wedding to the approval of Pembroke as mere jealousy of the opposite faction; and two days later, she became the bride of Honifort in York Minster, then in its first glory.

CHAPTER IV.

THE BEDESWOMAN.

'ONE castle could not hold two mistresses.' So said Sir Ferrand de Honifort.

Probably he also thought it could hardly have two masters; for he had received investiture of the Tower of the Meres, and done homage for it, as he told Blanche to make all things sure. As to offering ransom for Sir Thomas, he could not in conscience send good coin to the Scottish rebels. In less than a week, his lady had found that all the gold belonging to him was the clasp of his belt, nay, even that was pledged, and so was one of his black moustaches, which she had to redeem from a Lombard merchant before they could leave York. It was not for Scotland. He must first raise means from the churls. In France, people knew how to make Jaques Bonhomme pay, and not grow surly, as easiness made him here! So Blanche rode home in the trust that the six ruffianly-looking fellows in his train were the beginning of the band that was to uproot rebellion among the Scots, and bring home the heads of the two Bruces on the two points of a hayfork!

With ill-disguised vexation, he beheld the fond greeting of the sisters; and no sooner had he observed the complete obedience of the meinie of the castle to Ankaret, than he told his wife, loud enough to be heard by her sister, that nuns were best in their cells, and that it made him sick to see that white-faced devotee, for ever spinning save when she was telling her beads.

Blanche, who had begun to be possessed with a nameless fear of her lord, pleaded to keep her sister while he was pricking against the Scot; but she was told that he was waiting for the great expedition that the king was going to lead, so soon as he should have freed himself from the disloyal traitors who hindered him. She burst into tears, and said that such delays were not what she wedded him for; whereupon an evil look came into his small black eyes, and with uplifted arm he bade her beware of questioning the honour of a Honifort.

Ankaret saw that it would be better for all if she were away. Silent as she was, her presence inflamed Sir Ferrand, the retainers appealed to her against his commands, and not only they, but his wife, suffered when he had worked himself up into a true Gascon fury. So she told the weeping Blanche that she should leave her; and when her sister entreated that it might not be for so distant a cloister as Whitby, she said she should not enter a convent, as she could not give up her goods, till the ransom was paid.

'Alas!' sighed Blanche, 'my lord took thee at thy word, as to thy share of the lands.'

'I need no lands,' said Ankaret. 'There were three motherless lambs, which Gillian named after us three sisters, Nance, Blanche, and Jill. We bred them by the hall-fire, and now they graze on the hill-side. Those, and my own white goat, are all I would take with me, save what I have in my coffer.'

'Thy Book of the Hours,' said Blanche, carelessly; 'thou art welcome.'

'Somewhat more than that,' and Ankaret showed in the corner of the coffer a bag full of silver coins.

'I thought we had emptied our stores,' said Blanche. 'Didst thou keep back a hoard?'

'Nay, truly,' and Ankaret pointed to the distaff in her girdle. 'Dickon, the huckster, takes my yarn to the great chepe at York, and pays me for it in coined money. I hoard it towards the ransom,' and she smiled.

'Ah!' sighed poor Blanche, and then she whispered furtively, 'Let not my lord guess at it! Keep it in thy bosom, not thy coffer, when thou goest. And, oh! woe is me! Where wilt thou go?'

'Knowest thou not that the old anchoress, whose cell was in the wall of S. Oswald's, died last winter? By favour of the good parson, Sir Matthew, there mean I to abide, with my work and my beads.'

'Alas, how canst thou live?'

'My sheep and goat will graze on the hill-side, and there is an anchoress' croft which the good folks, of their charity, fill on the holy-days; also, they bring peats from the mountain. Fear not, sweet sister; I long for peace and rest.'

'There's little enough here,' moaned Blanche. 'Yet, didst thou spin night and day, what would that be towards the ransom? Alack, poor father!'

'It is my best,' said Ankaret. 'Spinning can do little, but God can do all. He bids us strive and pray, pray and strive; nor have I any other way of striving.'

'Woe is me, I strove without praying!' said Blanche.

'The way of prayer is never closed,' replied the elder sister.

So Ankaret repaired to one of the cells built for female hermits in the thickness of the church walls, with a scarce visible window and door outside, but a larger one of each into the Church. The anchoress could hear mass without quitting her cell, if she wished for total seclusion,; but if she became a lay sister of mercy to the parish, she opened her door and was easily accessible.

To Ankaret the cell was a blessed shelter and home, where she span and prayed, prayed and span, without distraction, living on goats' milk and barley cakes, which the goodwives of the dales left in plenty for the noble recluse, together with butter, cheeses, and mountain fruits; and fuel was willingly brought her by the peasants, also hay for the animals, which she housed in winter in a vault below her chamber. To a hardy North-countrywoman, trained in monastic rigour, there was nothing terrible in the cold, which made the temper of the Gascon knight so villanous that he nearly killed his wife, by throwing his heavy boot at her.

His temper was the worse for news of the fall of his patron, Gaveston, and for viewing poor Blanche as a connection of the Earl of Pembroke, one of the foremost in the overthrow; nor would he join the royal army the following year, because he professed not to be safe among Gaveston's enemies. The repulse the troops met was wholly due, he declared, to the absence of his doughty arm.

Then came a great Scottish invasion. It did not greatly affect the Lakes; for there was little promise of anything but hard blows in the mountain passes, and Honister Crag and Borrowdale Pass offered few temptations. So Blanche, from her battlements, and

Ankaret, from her church-tower, only beheld the sky lighted by distant flames, and prayed for the sufferers, as the horrid light went southwards; for Bruce swept on as far as Chester, and thence visited the Isle of Man, leaving his brother Edward to carry on the war in Scotland.

Edward Bruce was besieging Stirling, and had forced the governor, Mowbray, to pledge himself to yield unless he was relieved before Midsummer-day. Summonses to meet King Edward at Berwick were sent out to all his vassals, and a troop of gentlemen set forth with their yeomen for the muster, and among them Sir Ferrand de Honifort.

On the greensward of the ravine, at the head of which stood S. Oswald's Church, they encountered a small band of Scotsmen, coming from the north, all on horseback, and well armed. After the first shock, however, the enemy turned and fled from the larger and stronger body of English, as if they were leaderless, straight towards the Solway Firth, hotly pursued by the victors.

Ankaret had known nothing of this within the thick walls of her cell, murmuring her Psalms as she twisted her thread, until she was interrupted by the priest, Sir Matthew, who came to tell her that he needed her aid in dealing with a wounded man. She followed him to the northern end of the valley, where, on some rough ground hidden by fern and heather, beyond where the encounter had taken place, lay a man, senseless, in bright but plain armour. They loosed his helmet, and disclosed a sunburnt, rugged face of rufous complexion, a short beard, and hair of the same ruddy tint.

'A Scot!' exclaimed the priest, with some recoil.

'A Scot has a life to save,' said Ankaret. 'He seems to be only stunned. If we can shelter him from the people till night, he could, maybe, get over the Border.'

'Look you, daughter,' said the parson; 'I would gladly save any man's life; but a false Scot is not to be trusted with the knowledge of our lurking-places.'

Ankaret did not reply. She was putting wine to the knight's lips. He drank, looked at her with dazed eyes, and asked where were his loons.

'Do not speak, sir,' she said. 'You have been thrown, and your horse has run off. Can you walk a few paces to shelter and sanctuary?'

Still too much stunned for clear understanding, the Scot let himself be assisted to rise and move forward between the priest and Ankaret. At first he was too giddy to see or hear; but before they reached the Church he began to glare fiercely about him, to utter imprecations against his horse for stumbling and his men for deserting him, and to shake off his supporters.

'Trust us, sir,' said Ankaret. 'The Church is the only refuge from the dalesmen's knives.'

'How do I know that I may trust thee?' hotly demanded their prisoner.

'Because I am Ankaret d'Estouteville!' was the answer.

He was instantly silent, and went on with them to the Church. The dalesmen respected sanctuary; but their forbearance would be so sorely tried by knowing a Scottish foe to be near that it was thought best to dispose of the stranger in the vault where Ankaret stabled her sheep; and having left him there with a promise of fetching him food, Sir Matthew demanded of the lady whether she knew the man. She made a sign of assent, adding, 'But, dear sir, suffer me to hold my peace. It may be the better if questions be put to thee. Enough that now, if ever, I see hopes for my father.'

Sir Matthew had great trust in the noble anchoress, and, though a true lover of England, had no desire to see a gallant gentleman either murdered by dalesmen or given up to die as a traitor; so he consented to keep watch as he recited his breviary in the Church, while Ankaret carried provisions to the vault, in whose narrow bounds her captive was pacing like a panther in a cage, so that the clang of his armour was plainly audible above. She raised her hand, and warned him that his safety depended on being unheard. 'Safety!' he repeated. 'Means that captivity or freedom?'

'Thou knowest, Edward Bruce,' she answered. 'None, save myself—not even the parson—guesses thy name. We will do our best to speed thee over the Border safely, and I trust to the honour of the Bruces too much to think it needful to bind thee to the exchange.'

'Aha! thou hast a kindness for the traitors still!' said the rough Edward. 'Is't true that thou hast forsworn wedlock for poor Nigel's sake? Nay, I meant not to gar thee greet. Better for thee that thou wast not wed, or thou mightest be in an iron cage, like Robin's poor gudewife, who has had little joy of her queendom. Look ye! Dinna greet like that, mine old playmate. I'm not so ill a man as you English deem me. I should have driven my lance home, and never cried "Yield!" when I had stout Sir Thomas down, but for a thought of that merry Yule-tide, ere Rob became a hunted king instead of a merry earl; and then Rob laid on so weighty a ransom—in all honour to thy father's valour, mark'st thou! But I'll have my will for once; and Rob himself cannot gainsay that a king's brother is a fair exchange for a knight.'

He further explained that he had set out by the swiftest route to meet his brother returning from Man, and concert plans with him for the defence of the kingdom, intending to avoid notice. This had been disconcerted by the chance encounter with the English troop. Even before the charge, his stumbling horse had deprived his men of their leader, so that they had fled home, panic-stricken and deserted.

'My prisoner is mine own,' he repeated, 'and I may do as I will with him; but, to content Rob, I shall bind him over to bear no arms in this coming fight. If I deem rightly, it will do his fame no harm to be out of the fray that is at hand. Since Edward's death you have such a set of leaders that Hector of Troy himself could avail you little. So, if thou canst speed me on the way, thou shalt keep Beltane with him.'

That night Sir Edward Bruce, clad as a friar, set forth for the Solway, and, before Midsummer, Sir Thomas rode up the steep leading to his own castle, and beside him, on a little pony, a blooming and graceful maiden, in whom the sisters hardly recognised their wild Gillian.

'Child,' said he, as Ankaret knelt for his blessing, 'I should rather call on thee to bless me. Talk of sons to maintain a man's cause! My daughters have all been true and leal, but thou, Ankaret, hast done more than ten sons for me!'

'It was God's blessing on my poor prayers,' she said.

'Thanks and blessings be to Him,' said the knight. 'Only, my wench, I would thou hadst not let me be tied by yon plaguey condition! My hand itches for my lance; and they are gathering for such a field as there has not been since the fight of Falkirk.'

'Fie, father!' cried Gillian. 'Fight with our good friends and hosts?'

'All in good fellowship, minion. But Blanche's lord, Sir Ferrand, must do his devoir in the name of the Meres.'

The sisters rejoiced in his detention; and, when sad stragglers came home from Bannockburn, he owned that he had little to regret. Among them came not Ferrand de Honifort. Some said he had last been seen tumbling over his horse's neck as it trod into a calthorp; and Pursuivant Dutton, on his way home from his doleful task of identifying the slain, brought Blanche a fragment of a surcoat, in which she recognised her own embroidery; and thenceforth she believed her Knight of the Swan to have been all he professed when he came forward in her cause. Her father had made her very happy by declaring that her notion of her knight setting out at once on his own account had been foolish and impossible; and she recurred to her entire faith in her Gascon Paladin; tearfully recounted the mighty deeds she had on the best authority, namely, his own; and firmly believed, moreover, that it was his lance which had brought Edward Bruce to the ground, and that thus he had been the real deliverer of her father.

They let her alone in the belief that took away the sting of her sorrow. Gillian, who would have been the most likely to disabuse her, was far too happy to trouble herself in the matter; for Gilbert Dutton had come to propose an alliance between the families in the persons of herself and his grandson.

And so it was that Maurice Dutton became a worthy maintainer of the good old house of Estouteville, and Gillian's boys and girls were the delight of old Sir Thomas's heart, though he ever told them that no lad nor lass of them all would ever be worth their Aunt Ankaret, who still span, and still prayed, but in the fair convent of Whitby, instead of S. Oswald's cell.

There, in the Church, stood for two centuries a richly-carved shrine, on which had been spent the proceeds of Ankaret's spinning, as a thank-offering for her father's deliverance, while to many a worshipper it served as a memorial that the very weakest can win all things by the united power of faithful prayer and effort.

KASPAR'S SUMMER DREAM;

OR,

NOBLESSE OBLIGE.

G

KASPAR'S SUMMER DREAM.

> I could not love thee, dear, so much,
> Loved I not honour more.

'IT will be vain. Master, we shall but wreck ourselves. The hounds are behind us.'

'Think of the drag a set of helpless women will be on us!'

'We have beasts to set them on, for that matter!'

'Aye, and our merchandise?'

'Weigh merchandise in the scale with the lives of holy women! I speak for my father! He would rather lose every ounce of wool in his warehouse than let a hair of their heads be touched.'

'Meinherr Kaspar talks of he kens not what. If——'

'If,' said the first speaker, 'we tarry to bandy words, we shall save neither ourselves nor the nuns. To the vote be it! Hold up hands. Do we hurry to shelter at once, or do we warn the nuns and take them with us?'

It was a terrible question, for it was the year 1525.

They were Flemish merchants on their way from the great fair of Dantzig, with a long string of pack-horses and mules laden with furs, agates, and amber. Not twenty miles behind them raged the fanatic peasantry of Münzer, and in the wooded valley below the ridge on which they were travelling lay Marienhulf, a little secluded priory of nuns, certain to be the prey of the maddened wretches, and to suffer unspeakable horrors if they fell into their hands.

Hands were counted of the five merchants, and some dozen of the chief men in charge of the baggage. Eight for hastening on, nine for warning the nuns. Some of the eight murmured that Kaspar Vorstein was a mere lad, with no right to decide on men's lives, and that Peter Kuper had no right to a voice; but the Burgomaster Rossfeldt gave no more opening for discussion, but took the way down the road which led down the hill to the little convent.

It was like the stillness before a thunderstorm. The shingle-covered spire peered above the chestnut trees, the vine covered the walls, the homely brown stone building seemed to bask in quiet sunshine, all unaware of the imminent peril. The portress stared to see the cavalcade, and would rather have asked questions than have called the Prioress. The Burgomaster found it hard to make her understand that the heretic peasants, mad as wolves, would soon be on them. 'Ah! what harm have we done them? We have bound their wounds! we have given them soup! we have taught their children!'

Alas! little did the furious host reck of such benefits. Rossfeldt had to tell her fearful tales of murder and torture ere she would hearken, and even then the Prioress herself spoke words about martyrdom in the house in her own charge; but she thought of the tender maidens round her, and consented, even as some of those left to watch on the hill hurried to tell of fresh outbursts of smoke in villages nearer.

If the holy Mothers were coming at all, come they must, instantly. Too much time had been lost already. No farewell could be attempted. The nuns and their pupils, some five-and-twenty in number, could only be almost snatched up, and placed on the mules, leaving all their gear behind them, weeping and wailing amid the murmurs and oaths of many of the Flemings, who foresaw utter ruin and destruction in this freak of the Burgomaster and Kaspar Vorstein.

Happily, the nuns did not understand the language in which the threats were uttered. Neither did they perceive how, as the road became steep, and the beasts distressed, Kaspar and the men under his authority quietly cut the ropes which bound the packs, and let them fall off. On, on, through the forests and over the hills of Thuringia, were they struggling; and even when they reached a rising ground where they could see over the tree-tops, there were more burning villages and nearer! The Flemings were at least fifty in number, and armed to the teeth, but they avoided villages when it was possible, though those they passed seemed deserted. Only here and there a grim charcoal-burner, with an axe over his shoulder, scowled at them, and skulked past, evidently on his way to have a share of the spoil.

By-and-by it was plain that the enemy was gaining on them. The men of the party noted the curl of smoke from the double-cleft hill, beneath which the Priory of Marienhulf had stood, but would not point it out to the women. Perhaps the spoil there would detain the plunderers till there would be time to reach the shelter of the walls of Eulenberg. But the beasts were growing weary: there were sounds upon the air of yells and cries: the women asked no more questions: the men set their faces, and kept silence. They were about to go down the last hill into the open, bare plain, when, on the summit behind them, was seen the unmistakable dark mass of people—the multitude —broken, confused, irregular, easily to be destroyed by a regular army, but able to crush entirely that small troop of Flemings, who, on the road, now white and treeless, must be visible to them!

'Courage,' cried the Burgomaster, 'only one league yet to Eulenberg!'

Those who had objected to the care of the women were already far in advance; the remainder, cumbered as they were, hurried on. It was absolute flight along the road, smoother and better, but sandy, and choking with dust the failing beasts. There was nothing but a downhill rush now for the peasants to overtake them! Already their shouts had been heard at the sight of such a prey as were riding on at their best speed, when, in a sudden bit of broken ground, the mule of one of the nuns stumbled—fell—rolled over. Two alone saw the fall, and drew up—one a young girl, the other Kaspar Vorstein, who was riding last, with a pistol ready in his hand.

Both with one impulse were off their animals, freeing the nun from the mule, and trying to help it to rise. 'It cannot! its work is done,' said Kaspar. 'Ride on, lady. Reverend Mother, mount behind me.'

His trained horse stood by him faithfully; but the maiden's animal had followed its companions, and was already far off.

'Take her! take her, the Lady Ediltrude!' cried the nun. 'No matter for me; I am old! Go, my child!'

But Ediltrude clung to her. 'Never! I will

never leave thee, Sister Veronica. Save her; save her, sir.'

The horrible cries—the sound of trampling and rushing came nearer.

'I will take care of the good Mother. Mount, lady,' said Kaspar; 'my horse is fleet. You, gracious Lady, can quickly overtake the rest.' And he would have lifted Ediltrude into the saddle, but she dashed aside his hand, drawing herself up passionately.

'I—I fly, and leave others to die for me! I—a daughter of Sachs-Odinstein. All must be saved, or none!' And her blue eyes flashed, as she stood as like a rock as a slender maiden could stand.

'It might be too late now;' and in one second of thought, Kaspar decided that the insurgents would hurry on in pursuit of the main body, so that to swerve aside and lie concealed would serve best for him and the women. The sudden turn in the road, round a large stone, overshadowed by a tree, had probably hidden them, and he saw that a fence and ditch enclosed a field. Without a word he let his horse go, giving it a sign by which it knew it was to trot away. He could not at such a moment even sigh for the faithful creature. He merely whispered his plan to the two ladies, threw the grey lining of his cloak over Sister Veronica's black robes, made them descend with him into the ditch, and creep along to where it was overgrown with rank weeds.

Plunged among these, waving over their heads, the three sat in the damp, the two women in each other's arms, whispering prayers—the man with pistol in hand and sword across his knees. There they sat, and heard the host pass by. It was but a small portion, in truth, but the trampling of feet, the shouts, the yells, the cries of all kinds, the broken singing of hymns, the blasts of horns seemed endless. Once, when a step came nearer, Ediltrude held out her hand, and said, 'The other pistol, sir;' and he gave it.

Again her eyes glittered with strange light, her cheeks glowed, and, as her hair fell round her, her white-feathered head-gear having been torn off, Kaspar, even in those terrible moments, beheld her wondrous beauty. Still they crouched, none coming nearer; the steps grew fewer, the sounds more distant; yet, cramped, wet, and shivering as they were, they durst not move, lest stragglers should be in sight. They heard a dull booming of cannon, and sharper shots. Eulenberg must be firing on the enemy. Twilight began to fall. Kaspar stood up; Ediltrude followed his example. Nothing was to be seen, but it was dark enough to venture to move, and they dragged out poor Sister Veronica, stiff, chilled, and hardly able to stand, and crept back to the more open ground. Distant sounds and an occasional shot convinced Kaspar that the peasants were lying round Eulenberg, and that their way thither was cut off. He told the ladies that he thought the wisest way would be to get back within the forest. He remembered an empty charcoal-burner's hut, and thought there would be others where shelter might be found till the wild army had gone on its way. They assented, but poor Sister Veronica, as she tried to climb the hill, panted with sobbing breath and halting pace. She had been badly bruised in her fall, and could hardly walk, even when the young people supported her on either side. Again she bade them leave her to the Holy Mother and the Saints; again Ediltrude repeated that none born of Sachs-Odinstein would do so base a deed. At that moment the clatter of hoofs approached. Kaspar's ever-ready pistol was raised, when, just ere he fired, a low whinny was heard, and he cried, 'Star! my good Star, is it thou?' and as the good horse's white-starred forehead showed in the darkness, and it laid its nose lovingly on his shoulder, he added, 'Now, ladies, will all be well! We merchants ride not all unprovided;' and from beside his holster he drew out a small flask and a piece of bread and sausage, little enough, indeed, but even a mouthful was enough to revive the nun, and to strengthen Ediltrude's voice.

Star must carry the nun. Her faint protests died away as she was raised in Kaspar's arms; though she would at that moment, poor thing, have been well content to lie on the ditch side, hap what might, rather than be placed on horseback, though the Fleming supported her there, holding her in the saddle, and assuring her of the quietness of 'Star of Ypres;' but she had the great merit of patient silence, and Ediltrude walked on bravely beside her, rejoicing in the gathering darkness. The moon did not rise till they were within the wood, now entirely deserted, except for the rustle of a prowling animal here and there, which made the women tremble and press closer to their guardian.

At last they came to the hut, standing under a great pile of faggots, and, as Kaspar expected, perfectly lonely and deserted. 'You may rest here safely, dear ladies,' he said; 'the fellow who harbours here will scarce return for many a day, if at all.'

The nun, with a sigh of relief, was lifted down, and Ediltrude ran into the house, joyfully proclaiming that here was a cat, and a goat, and a kettle—aye, and all man could want, hens even, and no doubt eggs!

The immediate danger over, the spirit of adventure and a pleasant sense of freedom seemed to have seized on the maiden, for while Kaspar provided for the wants of his horse from a heap of lately-cut hay, and the nun sank on her knees before a rude Crucifix, she ran about making discoveries; the cat impeding her by rubbing itself against her feet, and the goat bleating to be milked, both creatures evidently having been miserable in their desertion. The hut must have belonged to a somewhat well-to-do forester, for it had two chambers, the inner one with a straw bed, and the outer one with two chests, one of coarse meal, the other of clothes. So much the moonlight had shown Ediltrude, when Kaspar came in, with the brand he had kindled at the fire, which he knew the charcoal-burner would have left to smoulder under his pile. It was a warm evening in summer, and fire was not needed, except to toast the eggs which had been found near the roost where the hens had proclaimed them, and which served the party for their supper, with some milk drawn by Ediltrude's hands, not without mirth, as Kaspar held the goat for her, marvelling at the dexterity of the soft, little, unaccustomed fingers.

He assured the ladies that they might sleep safely in the inner room while he kept watch, and Sister Veronica trusted him all the more, when he joined with them in the devotions of the evening hour, making the responses in much better Latin than she knew, and with a readiness which made her observe at the end, that the gracious gentleman prayed like a divinity scholar, to which Kaspar replied that the holy fathers had good schools at Ghent.

The nun and her pupil slept the sleep of excessive fatigue, and when they awoke and came forth from their very small and gloomy den, they were startled at first by the apparition of a figure in the peasant dress, rough dark-blue homespun guarded by untanned leather; but the bow and greeting reassured them in a moment. Kaspar had thought it wise to make free with the Sunday clothes of the master of the hut, and having found a bundle of feminine gear, advised the ladies to do the same. He said he had money enough about him to make full compensation to the owners.

'Ah, sir! and what will ever make compensation to you?' cried Ediltrude.

'It is enough for me if I have saved you,' was his answer, with an eager look passing over his face; then tendering to her a large bowl of water, he added, 'I have found the good man's arrows, and slain a rabbit; I will make it ready for the cooking, while the gracious ladies change their dress.'

'Ah!' cried Ediltrude as he moved away, 'when would a German have shown such courtesy? Did you ever see one so goodly or so noble, dear mother?'

Poor Sister Veronica assented, though she was very

miserable about the change of dress, which was such a dreadful irregularity as no Sister of Marienhulf had ever been guilty of; but she was forced to submit, while Ediltrude danced about in absolute delight at the fun of arraying her as an old woman, with dark blue gown, bright apron, and white hood, tied down with a red kerchief, comparing her in turn to all the old women who haunted the gates of the convent.

Ediltrude herself was soon clad in much the same costume, only with head bare of all but its own light brown hair, which she plaited in two long tails, and allowed to hang down her back. In this masquerading garb she darted out at the door, and made a splendid curtsey to the seeming peasant, demanding how he approved of 'Trüdchen, the woodman's daughter.'

For all answer, he took off his cap, and with a deep red mounting in his cheek, bowed to her very feet.

Yes, Kaspar Vorstein was a noble-looking youth, not only tall, straight, and easy of bearing, like one well trained, but with thought, depth, and force in his clear, frank, dark eyes, and the mould of his mouth and chin just marked by the young moustache of the earlier years after twenty. And his was not the courtesy of court training, but true delicate consideration towards the two helpless women for whom he had perilled himself already. In the council held over the morning meal, the contriving of which was sport to the maiden, he advised them to tarry where they were for at least that day, while the provisions sufficed them! Since the open country was dangerous, from the parties of peasants who would be plundering there, even if beaten off by Eulenberg, and on any token of danger it would be easy to hide in the wood.

The resolution was adopted, nor did any peril approach the trio. Kaspar reconnoitred from a tree on the outskirts of the forest, and saw curls of smoke that told of other burning abbeys and granges, and he counselled another day of concealment. The nun was nothing loth. Poor thing, she was stiff, bruised, exhausted, and felt the quiet a respite; and as to Ediltrude, it was the most charming holiday she ever had in her life, in that green wood, in all its summer glory, with the thousand flowers at her feet, and the playing at homely occupations, with that devoted Kaspar to save her from all that was rough and troublesome, and he evidently impressed and charmed with all she achieved.

Kaspar Vorstein was a very different being from all she had known or heard of. Son of a wealthy cloth merchant of Ghent, he had been bred in all the scholarship and cultivation of the golden age of the Netherlands, had a nature trained by books, an eye by art, a tongue, by converse with men of all nations, and by travel in several countries, even to Italy and Spain. Sister Veronica heard with delight of the shrines at which he had prayed, and thought herself repaid for all her trials when she kissed his rosary, blest by the Pope—the good Flemish Pope Adrian—who had once, when tutor to the Emperor, given his blessing to Kaspar as a boy in Ghent.

Day after day passed, and still it was plainly unsafe to venture from the shelter of the forest. Kaspar, when he had arranged a retreat for the ladies, and found that Ediltrude at least would let him leave her without too much terror, for an hour, went down, confident in his disguise and his knowledge of German, to learn the state of things and buy provisions. The peasants were collecting constantly in large numbers round Münzer's ensign, the golden shoe, and there were stories, too horrible to tell his charge, of their usage of monks, nuns, knights, and ladies, on all of whom they were wreaking the vengeance of years of grinding oppression, with the brutal, stolid cruelty of the German peasant. Eulenberg's walls had resisted them, but they filled the country round, gradually tending however towards Frankenhausen. Thus, neither to Eulenberg, nor to any other sufficient shelter, was the way open.

After all, were the young people very sorry to

have it so? Were not these long days in the good greenwood full of untold enjoyment to the convent-bred maid, when she milked the goat, gathered the eggs, fed the chickens, or stirred the meal, or when she gathered the flowers to weave into wreaths to lay at the foot of the Crucifix, or sat on the grass listening to Kaspar's replies to her questions about the great Flemish towns, and the noble Churches, grand paintings, splendid processions, and great men, that were to him constant sights! She had little drawback in her enjoyment. There was hardly a doubt that her friends of the Convent were safe in Eulenberg; and she was an orphan who had spent her life there ever since her mother's death, and had only once or twice seen her father, who three years since had fallen in an Italian battlefield; so she had no one to care for nearer than the Prioress, a distant cousin, under whose care she had been placed. Of course those happy days were rendered the deeper, the richer, the sweeter, by a feeling which the maiden understood as little as simple-hearted Sister Veronica was able to perceive those tokens which a secular eye would have noted long ago. Yet Kaspar Vorstein, as he became conscious of what made him rejoice in every report which prolonged this woodland sojourn, felt less doubt and fear than might have been expected.

Flemish burghers, under their countryman Charles

of Ghent, ranked high in power and esteem; and though he knew Ediltrude was noble, the orphan daughter of a penniless Saxon lord was no unfitting mate for one who could count burgomasters and provosts among his forefathers as long as Ghent had stood, had wealth enough in his family to buy up a hundred Saxon baronies, and, young as he was, already stood high in the guild of cloth-workers.

And so, when he had heard in the neighbouring village a report that the insurgents had been routed at Frankenhausen by the Landgraf of Hesse and the Duke of Brunswick, and had been slaughtered like sheep with ferocity equal to their own; he felt that it was time to leave the forest before any stragglers should return in the madness of revenge; but he did not feel that he need yet wake from his summer dream. It seemed to him a good omen that when he came to the hut, he found Ediltrude with her lap full of forget-me-nots from the brook, which she was weaving into a garland.

There is no need to say how each anticipated the other's thought that never would these days be forgotten, nor how the tenderness of his eyes even more than his words awoke the full perception in Ediltrude's heart that he was to her, all, and more than all, that ever knight of song or tale was to lady—her Parzeval, her Hildebrand, her Siegfried!

He had told her of his grave, wise father, and gentle, dignified, housewifely mother, in the grand old house with high gables and many windows, and the wide, dark-timbered, polished hall with the winding staircase; and now he pleaded with her to come home with him, and be their child, and share the citizen life that seemed already to her so rich and sweet and fair with all life's best. He knew, indeed, that he was beneath her.

'Oh no! wiser, better, truer than any I ever knew!' and the eyes gazed into his, and the hand stole into his clasp. 'Oh! it would be happiness!'

'Then tell me, sweet love, canst thou give thyself to me, when we can find a priest?'

'So truly would it be best. Then none would gainsay us.'

'Is there any that would have the right? Must I ask thee of any?'

'Oh, no! I do not own the right of any over me,' she said. 'My father is dead. None can bind me—I am surely my own.'

There was a sort of assertion and defiance in her tone that made him uneasy, and he reiterated the question—

'Thou hast no kinsman—no claim to which thou owest thyself?'

'None like thee! None like him to whom I owe

life and love, and more. I freely—oh! how freely—give all up for thee!'

'Tell me, my own lady, what dost thou give up for the poor burgher?'

'So! just the old castle and Duchy.'

'Duchy?'

'Yea, the Duchy of Sachs-Odinstein. Thou dost not seek after it, my Kaspar, dost thou? The castle is grim and ruinous, and there are such strange howlings in the galleries!'

'Thou art Duchess of Sachs-Odinstein?'

'Yes, of course. Didst not know it? My cousin, the Elector, has managed it since my blessed father and brothers died in Italy, and he may manage it still, unless he will give it to Albrecht Wilhelm.'

'Who is Albrecht Wilhelm?' said Kaspar, growing more gloomy.

'Albrecht Wilhelm! It is he to whom my father promised me and my dukedom; but be not afraid, Kaspar. He is forty years old, and has lost one eye, and is terrible to look at. Father brought him to Marienhulf once to see me, and give me this ring; but it was five years ago, and I cried, and the Mother Prioress whipped me for it when they were gone.'

'Thou art promised to another?' he cried, with a look of despair and agony on his face,

'But not by my own will. Kaspar, I vow myself to——'

He interrupted her by a gesture of command, as if from exceeding pain—almost horror—that he could hardly endure; and she stopped, alarmed. There was a dead pause, while he hid his face in both hands, and she looked at him with wide-open, terrified eyes. At last he uncovered his face, entirely altered in expression, drew a long breath, and said—

'It has been a summer dream. Her Highness must forgive me.'

'Away with Highness! away with dukedoms and all the rest! I hate them!' cried the girl passionately. 'Take me to Flanders. What? art afraid?' she added, with infinite scorn in her voice.

'Yes, lady, afraid of a broken vow and a dishonourable action, or of living a lie, as we must do, unless we would bring vengeance on my city and family.'

She sat with clasped hands looking fixedly at him, her bosom heaving with emotion. Presently she murmured—

'Thou saidst thou didst love me.'

'Love thee! Heaven knows how much! I love thee so much, lady, that I would not soil thy perfect truth and honour, nor mine own. That were not love, lady; it would be baseness.'

'And thou wilt leave me to hard, iron-handed, one-eyed Albrecht?' moaned Ediltrude; 'me, who would have given up all for thee.'

'Nay, not thy father's plighted word. Listen, lady; I know how it is with you princes. You may not live and die for yourselves. You have people under you, and you must act for them. I have heard of this Duke Albrecht Wilhelm the one-eyed—nay, I have seen him in the Emperor's train. He is a good man and true, and will not deal amiss.'

'Hush!' broke in the poor girl. 'How dare you?—I cannot bear it. See now, let him have my lands. All will deem me taken and slain by the peasants. They will say masses for me, and write "Ediltrudis ob. 1522" in the family tree, and none will miss me, nor need any know in Ghent that I ever was aught but the maid whom thou didst save.'

Kaspar shook his head.

'The faithful burgher may not steal a wife,' he said. 'No, Serene Lady, thou knowest not what thou sayest. Forgive me when thou dost awaken to the knowledge.'

The sad gravity, with which he bowed, bared his head, and moved away, awed her too much for her to follow him, and she gave way to bitter weeping and framing of wild schemes, which looked possible and plausible at one moment, then collapsed again at the thought of Kaspar's countenance. At last Sister Veronica came to her, found out what was the matter, and was thunderstruck, laying all the blame on Kaspar. Who could have thought of such wickedness and presumption in a young man who could make all the responses in the Hours as well as the precentrix herself? But all men were evil, and when once out of this dreadful wood, Sister Veronica hoped never to speak to another save her father confessor. Fighting Kaspar's battles, albeit all in vain, did somewhat restore Ediltrude. One question she longed to ask, but the evening passed by, and the burgher did not come in to supper, and was seen nowhere.

The good mother began to be seriously alarmed lest Ediltrude should have actually driven him away; but after much restlessness and terror, she looked forth and detected his dark outline, wrapped in his cloak, leaning against the wall of the house, which he was watching as a sentinel.

He came forward as he perceived her, and in a low tone, so sunken and altered that she hardly knew it, explained to her that the time was come for descending into the open country, and making their way to Meissen, where the Lady Duchess Ediltrude might be delivered to the head of her family, the Elector.

He thought that if the gracious ladies could be ready, it would be best to depart at daybreak.

Always obedient, Sister Veronica assented, and tried to persuade him to come in for food and rest; but he thanked her, and said he wanted nothing, and would rather watch outside. The notion of the need of watching filled her with renewed terror, and she sat up, nodding in her chair all night, while Ediltrude sobbed herself to sleep, torn, poor child, by many a strange, new feeling, in which began to predominate above disappointment, wounded love, and indignation, together with a dread lest Kaspar should be despising her for wishing what he thought unworthy.

The morning came, the last meal was eaten in haste and silence, gold enough for ample compensation was placed on the table, food was left within reach of the animals, and the charcoal-burner's hut was left, Kaspar leading the horse, and the nun mounted on it, since she and Ediltrude were to ride by turns.

Scarcely a needless word had passed, but the two young people's eyes met as they turned for a last look at what each one's heart declared to have been where their happiest days had been passed.

It was then that Ediltrude ventured on the question she had been longing to ask.

'Is it because I am a duchess, or because I am promised?'

'Because your Highness is promised,' he said, as briefly as he could.

He never omitted the title now, as if to mark the space between them. He looked pale, downcast, and sad, like a man who had steadfastly passed through a great tempest.

Once more she spoke.

'We will commit it to my cousin Friedrich.'

And then Sister Veronica, who had been vowing penances on her foolish, blind, unwatchful self for having ever left the two young people to their own mischievous devices, was seized with a desire to walk, and insisted on getting down.

Kaspar was aware that there was no reasonable hope of 'Cousin Friedrich' making a decision in his favour, but he knew the wise Elector Friedrich to be a man not as other men are, more generous, more liberal-minded, more conscientious; and the fragment of hope, though he despised its folly, buoyed him up on the way to Meissen, through a desolated country, where Abbey and Church had been sacked and burnt by the insurgents; and even more recently the villages and hamlets of the rioters had been furiously ravaged by the nobility and their men-at-arms, both sides alike with deadly wrongs to avenge.

Sister Veronica shuddered, wept, and prayed silently as they passed the ruins, or the more terrible sight of unburied corpses by the wayside. The stress of personal feeling—it can hardly be called suspense—was too strong upon Kaspar for conscious feeling of what he saw; but his eye took it in, and his memory was imprinted with all, in a passive way, which perhaps for that very reason was deeper; while Ediltrude's most defined sensation was of desire to prolong the present—a feeling akin to that of a truant who must fall into severe hands when once more within bounds, but, above all, did she dread losing the presence of Kaspar, changed as he was.

They fell in by-and-by with a party of horsemen, bearing a banner with the black and gold bars and green bend of the princely Saxon families, and Kaspar saw it was the only safe course to lead his little party straight up to them, if he wished to save his party from being shot down as peasants escaping with their spoil.

Even as they advanced, muskets were levelled at them, and possibly the perception that the horse was worth having was their chief protection from being fired upon, without enquiry, by the first reckless landsknechts who had caught sight of them.

'Hold, fellows!' shouted Kaspar. 'This is the Duchess Ediltrude of Sachs-Odinstein! Fetch your leader.'

There was a shout of laughter.

'We know better than that. Duchess Ediltrude was slain at Marienhulf——.'

'Knaves that ye are, silence!' said Ediltrude, holding herself upright in her saddle. 'I forbid you to touch this gentleman!'

Her face and gesture made the landsknechts hold back and presently perceive that she was indeed the Duchess. An officer came up saluting her respectfully as she said—

'Lead us to my kinsman, sir,' while she took good heed that Kaspar Vorstein should hold her bridle.

Before they had gone many steps she was hailed by a large, heavy man on horseback—

'Ha, my little cousin, we had given thee up for lost! This will be good news for Albrecht! How didst escape the ruffians?'

'By means of this gentleman, Sir Cousin Johann,' replied Ediltrude, with defensive dignity. 'Herr Kaspar Vorstein, of Ghent, whom I commend to your especial care. Herr Vorstein, I present you to Duke Johann.'

'So? A fine squire of dames. Look to him, Rambold,' said Johann of Saxony gruffly, as he scanned Kaspar's fair, youthful face.

Netherlanders were viewed with much dislike and jealousy as favourites of the Emperor; and only the certainty, that any outrage on one of them would be severely punished, protected Vorstein. The young lady's evident solicitude did him rather harm than good; but he was unmolested, though watched like a prisoner by the Saxons, who thought it presumption in a mechanical Fleming to have rescued their young lady, and worse presumption still to be young and handsome.

Of course there was no more speech for him with Ediltrude, though at the first halt Duke Johann, the Elector's brother and heir, came towards him and said, employing the second person plural, as used by nobles towards inferiors, where there was no familiarity:

'I understand, Master Vorstein, from the Serene Lady and from the holy Mother, that you have protected them, and conducted yourself towards them with respect. Our family is obliged to you, and the Elector will consider your claims.'

Kaspar's spirit glowed so hotly that it well nigh burst forth into flame, though he forced himself to keep back all words save—

'As to claims, your Highness, I make none. Man is bound to defend woman.'

'The house of Saxony knows its obligations,' said Johann, coldly, taking perhaps offence at the mention of a daughter of that house as a woman, or else gathering an impression of suppressed fervour in the young man's look; for when he returned to the ladies he spoke of 'the insolence of these Flemish knaves.'

Ediltrude broke forth, 'Never did I see knight or junker so courteous as he.'

'Courteous? So! Mayhap too courteous! What will Albrecht say to that, my lady?'

'I hate Albrecht,' muttered the girl.

'So! So!' again exclaimed Duke Johann. 'How now, Duchess Ediltrude? A little more of this, and I shall think my jest earnest, and find a tree and a noose for the upstart weaver who has dared to turn thy silly head. Well for him that Albrecht is not here.'

The threat closed Ediltrude's lips in terror, infinitely dreading lest her outbreak should already have excited suspicion, and still more fearing what Sister Veronica might say in her simplicity, and what construction might be put on it. But fortunately Sister Veronica was so much shocked at finding herself in the hands of so well-known a Lutheran as Duke Johann that she never opened her lips if she could help it, except to murmur constantly a low whisper of the penitential Psalms so as to close her ears against the heretic conversation around.

So they rode to Meissen, where the good Elector, Friedrich the Wise, had his dwelling in a grand old mansion, half castle, but with more likeness to a hospitable burgher house.

Sister Veronica was dropped at a convent, where she hoped to rest apart from all those strange rude beings, men, till she could again regain her own community. Ediltrude cast one wistful glance as she was assisted from her horse, and met Kaspar's eye.

That was all. He saw her no more that evening, and was entertained with grave courtesy at a sort of second table of the Elector's, where supped stewards, comptrollers of the household, and the like, with a few students, and some reverend, acute-looking men, whom he supposed to be Lutheran teachers.

Saying as little as he could, and answering as few questions on the young Duchess's adventures as was possible without exciting suspicion, he found that there was great joy at her safety, and that Duke Friedrich, already in failing health, had been seriously ill from sorrow and anxiety on her account, grieving at having left in a nunnery, exposed to such danger, the orphan of one kinsman, the bride of another.

Yes, and it was spoken of as a strange weakness in the good Elector that he was actually mourning over the rascals of peasants—the rogues, the ruffians who had done such outrages—and saying it was on themselves, that the princes of the Empire should be taking vengeance for their own oppression; not on these sheep whom they themselves had transformed into wolves.

'All that came of Brother Martin's doctrine,' said a tight-capped be-ruffed, black-gowned housekeeper, shaking her head.

'Nay, Brother Martin was as keen against the rogues as any landsknecht of them all,' added another. 'Cut and slay was the best word he had for them when they came nigh the walls of Wittenberg.'

'The princely Elector hath not of late held in all things with Brother Martin since he came back from the Wartburg.'

Whereon a clamour arose, some declaring the Elector's perfect confidence in, and adherence to, Brother Martin, others declaiming on his mere sufferance of the meddling Augustinian, whose pride and obstinacy were the real cause of all the troubles.

Kaspar, too sad at heart to take his part in the controversy, soon ceased to listen when he had once gathered that the Elector looked on things in a fashion of his own, which those around him often found past their comprehension. He was glad that the decorous rules of the Electoral household caused the supper to end without the usual German excess; and though he was startled by hearing a chapter read aloud, ere the tables were removed, from Luther's newly-published New Testament in German, the beauty of the rendering of the sixteenth chapter of St. John sent him to his rest calmed and peaceful. It had to him only the novelty resulting from the new language, and from his own state of mind, for he had studied it both in the Vulgate and in Erasmus' version; but the 'yet a little while' seemed to win power over his heart and brain, and, worn out with wakeful nights and days of anxiety and emotion, he slept with '*über ein Kleines*' in his ears.

Mass was said in the Electoral chapel in the morning, for as yet there was no abandonment of the old ritual, save by such as Carlstadt, whose doings had not only brought Luther back from the Wartburg, but had opened the Elector's eyes to the tendency of what he had hoped for as the beginning of the purifying of the Church.

Not long after the solid breakfast which followed, came a summons to the Elector's chamber: the page who brought it looking round at Master Vorstein with a sort of sly curiosity and awe, as if the monkey had some inkling of the reason.

Friedrich, called the Wise, sat in a dark loose gown, trimmed with fur, in a pillowed chair, near the fire, which he needed even on that summer day. He had a noble head, bald, and with white locks behind, and a countenance of that beauty so notable in aged men of the Saxon race, even when the features have not been moulded and inspired by a soul such as that of Friedrich of Saxony. A blameless and stainless hero in his youth, full of religious enthusiasm, which even in that degenerate century had carried him to make his knighthood's vows beside the Holy Sepulchre; and in elder life he had been equally brave and merciful, and so loved and revered that he had been actually chosen Emperor; and only did not wear the crowns of Germany and Italy because he held that the lord of so small a hereditary state as his own was incapable of making head against the Turkish invaders who threatened Christendom. A sense of the evils of the Church system around him had made him foster and protect Luther, and provide for his safety after the Diet of Wurms; but the development of the doctrine of the reformer had greatly disappointed him, and while his brother and nephew accepted it eagerly, he was turning back to first principles, going far deeper than it was in their nature to do. He was, in fact, wasting away under his grief at the state of Christendom and the Empire, while his age and broken health forbade him to come forward.

Little did Kaspar Vorstein think of all this, or indeed perceive aught but that the Elector was alone, save for one young girlish figure at his side, her veil drawn forward, as if she had been weeping very bitterly.

The old man held out his hand, and the princely

courtesy of his greeting was a contrast to the proud roughness of his brother and followers.

'The dear Herr will pardon a sick man for not rising to thank him for being good enough to come to him.'

Constrained by the majesty of the gracious brow, Kaspar knelt on one knee and kissed the hand; then ventured on a silent kiss to a hand that hung near, and was moved towards him, while a dim, extravagant hope infinitely quickened his already throbbing heart.

'Yes,' said Friedrich, answering the gesture, 'the child has told me all, and how her defender acted like a true and faithful man, for which I heartily thank him.'

'And will his gracious Highness pardon the presumption of which only ignorance could make me guilty?' ventured Kaspar.

'Nay, an old man must needs know human nature enough to see that a youth and maiden can hardly be left to wander in the woods together—without feeling that minstrels spake the truth. Children,' he added, changing from his formality to the kindest, most fatherly tone, 'I blame you not, nay, I heartily pity you both. From what this maid tells me, Herr Kaspar, thou hast treated her as too few of our highest born would have done—with all the honour that I well know in the true and faithful burghers of the Netherlands. I would verily that I had the power to bid you both be happy. Were I in my strength and vigour, and were she wholly free, I could be tempted to let one, who has been trained to wider and juster views than are held by some of us, rule her dukedom and guard her vassals. But in the eyes of all those around, a Fleming burgher on the Ducal seat would be but a mark for insult and enmity. His very improvements would be hated and scorned by his own vassals, and Sachs-Odinstein, with its 700 men, could not stand against the whole force of Saxony. It would be death and shame to both of you, and ruin to the vassals whom she is bound to guard.'

They could not but make mute assent, and he proceeded: 'She has even besought me, the foolish child, to let her resign all and go with thee.'

He looked at Ediltrude, but her scheme did not seem to dissolve in confusion as the elder lips spoke it. She looked up in her tears and said, 'I would.'

'Yes, so thou mightest were it only the choice between the being princess of a poor little petty state, and housewife to a wealthy merchant that were for thy choice,' said the Elector; 'but thou art a born princess, and the duties of a princess must thou have to thy vassals whom God gave thee. Duke Albrecht is the fit man to have the charge of thee and of them, and thou canst not rob him nor them of what thy blessed father appointed. Wert thou away, seest thou not Albrecht, but Georg were the heir, and how would it be with thy people then? Maiden, thou seest thou art not thine own. Thy birth constrains thee! This good youth, thou sayest, had already perceived this, when he first knew thy rank! He sees that the kindest part he can act is to pass from thy sight, and let this summer vision fade like yonder rainbow.'

They both looked up, Ediltrude, through her tears, to the window, where over the woods to the northward the noonday sun had painted a bright arch on the passing shower.

'The rainbow,' murmured Kaspar almost to himself. 'The rainbow is fleeting, but eternal!' There was a look on his face that neither of them understood as he added, 'I thank your Highness for the token! Lady, fair and blessed lady, fare thee well. Forget. It is all I can ask of thee, and so shall I have done thee no harm. But bear away my thanks for the days of joy that nought can take from me——'

The Elector interposed, fearing perhaps that the young man might be betrayed into marring the effect of his resignation.

'That is enough, sir; Ediltrude, let him kiss thine hand and retire.'

They obeyed; their hearts might be bursting, but

they were silent and endured, while the door shut on Ediltrude.

Kaspar by a gesture craved dismissal, but the Elector held out his hand. 'A few words more, sir, if you can bear them. I grieve for you, sorely grieve; but you are too true a man not to know that all gives way to honour and to duty. Do not feel insulted, but forgive me if, as an old man and a friend, I ask you the favour of telling me if I can do anything for you.'

'Nothing, your Electoral Highness. There are merchants here who have traffic with my father, and will forward me on my way home.'

'That is well. And I need hardly say, as you said but now to the poor child, that I trust this dream will not have harmed thee. A noble love, whether its fate be prosperous or adverse, cannot harm a man, but must rather lead him higher.'

Years had come and gone. The Duchess Ediltrude had been a good and duteous, and fairly happy, wife to a brave and upright husband, who ruled her tiny principality on the lines of the good Elector. She was a beneficent princess and a good mother, and there was sorrow when in her age and widowhood, she resigned her rule to her eldest son, and went to dwell for a time with her daughter, who had married a Flemish nobleman.

She took her full grandmotherly share of the fears and joys of the family, when the sons were fighting in the armies of Philip II. One gained much honour at the battle of Lepanto, the other, the youngest and the darling of the family, with a fair German face that might have been a maiden's, was given up as lost. He was known to have been carried wounded to a farm-house, which on the next day, the troops had been forced to leave to the Dutch, and there had been no means of carrying him away.

But in the midst of the mourning, a letter arrived from the Prince of Orange, stating that young Marquis Albert was a prisoner, and fixing his ransom. The sum was raised, and in time the lad was brought home by boat and litter, pale, wasted, helpless, with a shattered limb, which had nearly cost him his life.

He was even then too weak and exhausted to reply to many questions. He only said something about having been saved by a good priest, who stayed by him when his fellow-soldiers were forced to leave him to the enemy; but, like many men who have seen and suffered much, he was slow to talk of what he had gone through.

One day, however, when he had been left alone with his grandmother, the nurse he liked best, there had been a sudden shower, and the setting sun was lighting up a magnificent rainbow on the dark cloud flitting away to the east. The Duchess Ediltrude let her hands drop on her lap, and sat gazing at it with a strange, rapt expression in her aged face. Young Albert lay and watched her, and at last he said, 'The Lady grandmother looks at the rainbow as did the good Father Kaspar.'

'Kaspar!' She breathed the word in a sort of gasp, and a youthful carnation spread over the pure though wrinkled pallor of her aged cheek. 'Kaspar! Was it he? Why did you never tell me!'

'I knew not how,' said Albert.

'And Kaspar saved thee,' she repeated. 'Did he know who thou wert?'

'At last, not at first, I think. See, grandmother, it was thus.' And the lad told how, in the defence of an outpost, he had been shot down, carried into a house and laid on a bed, whence it was not possible to move him when, the next day, the Duke of Alva had to retreat, for the bleeding had been so excessive that his life hung on a thread, and the slightest movement would have been death to him. All depended on perfect stillness, and food every half hour, and no one was willing to risk a life for a man as good as dead. He himself had known nothing of all this. It was not till after hours of faintness, followed by a long, refreshing sleep, that he woke to see that an aged priest was bending over him, and giving him wine.

During that day he rallied much in the stillness, and learnt the state of things. Being fully aware that the clergy ran especial danger from the Dutch Calvinists, he asked whether the Father had any pass from them. A smile and shake of the head was the answer, as if it mattered but little; and the priest went on to say, 'It is strange joy to me to do aught for one who bears that look and tone. Does not the gracious lord own some German kindred?' Then when Albert answered that his mother was a Sachs-Odinstein Felsen, to his amazement, the old man fell on his knees in thanksgiving. All the explanation he then gave was that he had known the Duchess in his youth. Then having once learnt that she was living and well, he spoke no more of the matter.

'But why not bring him hither? Would that I could see him, and tell him how his upright sense of duty has a thousand times guided and strengthened me! Why didst not bring him, Albert?'

'Alas, grandmother!' and Albert went on to tell how ere many hours were past, the Dutch were upon them, and how Father Kaspar forced on the knowledge of the first-comers that the wounded man was a son of the Marquis of Hautroncel, and a cousin of the Prince of Orange, well worth taking alive. But for himself, he was instantly recognised as the Jesuit Kaspar Vorstein, who had turned back so many converts to his Church again, and who was doubly detestable and dangerous because he was loved and praised by all who came under his influence.

Some were for shooting him down at once, but the most part were for reserving him for the Provost-Marshal, and for examination in case he should know any state secrets. These latter prevailed, and at the entreaty of Albert, and of the priest himself, he was allowed to continue at his post of nurse all night, sentries being placed to prevent his escape.

There was nothing about him by which the youth could have guessed that he well knew that examination meant torture. He was gravely kind and earnest as ever, and divided the night watches between prayer and care of the young man; but towards morning, seeing that Albert was awake, he spoke more, bidding him, when he should see the Duchess again, thank her for what she had been to himself through life, though unseen since that summer dream. Kaspar had vowed that no less noble bride should ever take her place. It had then been, as he said, a foolish vow of earthly disappointment, but it had led him to the thought of the Mystic Bride, the noblest of all. As he went home in his sadness to see her shrines overthrown, her Altars defiled, her votaries driven out, and all because her shepherds had fed themselves instead of the flock, and fouled the waters with their feet, a spirit of self-devotion to her cause took possession of him. He might not have the lady of his love, but the Church should be his lady.

How he gave up his wealth and traffic to his brother, and devoted himself to the priestly life. How his love passed even above the earthly Church to her Lord and Master in Heaven, he had scarcely told Albert; but many a voice could have said what he had been to the desolated country in his steadfast faith, untiring love, and brave rebuke of evil.

It was a stormy night, and the sun was rising behind the house, and painting a splendid rainbow on the western cloud. When the priest was summoned to be taken before the Prince of Orange, Albert had contrived to write on his tablets an earnest entreaty for his life and safety, to be given to the prince, and thus could bear to see him depart, in the hope of his return.

Father Kaspar had bent down and kissed his brow, crossed him, and blessed him, then said, 'I thank my Lord for this. Thou hast been one rainbow to me. He hath given me another yonder. The earthly one is fleeting. That about the Throne is for ever and ever.'

Albert never saw him more. The Prince of Orange durst not rescue a Jesuit from the hatred of the Dutch. But Albert's note had so far prevailed that there was no torture, and the death was sharp and sudden, which raised the self-devoted priest to the glorious army of martyrs.

So had the noble love led to a nobler, the love that was denied to the Love that never denies those who seek it!

BUY A BROOM.

CHAPTER I.

ENGLISH people naturally think of the Wood of Soignies in connection with the Battle of Waterloo, but my story is concerned with it nearly three hundred years before the time of that great victory, when the name of Belgium had not yet been revived, or more properly invented, and when Brussels was only known as the chief city of the duchy of Brabant. Soignies formed part of the great forest of Ardennes, the favourite hunting-ground of the Dukes, first of Brabant, and then of Burgundy. It was later much loved of the Emperor Charles V., who, though lord of so many nations, was most entirely a Fleming at heart and in language.

In some parts of the forest there were large trees and impenetrable thickets, but the greater portion consisted (as it does still) of broken ground, covered with scattered copsewood of holly and birch, with an undergrowth of fern and bracken, and glades of short grass between, affording pasturage for the deer, swine, and other animals of the chase that haunted the forest.

Lodges for the Emperor's foresters and woodmen were found at long intervals, one or two of them furnished with sylvan spoils and with conveniences for a night's rest, in case any of the princely huntsmen might wish to sleep there; and in the depths and glades there squatted a few other inhabitants. Some were outlaws, who preyed upon the deer, and eluded the pursuit of the keepers; and others were woodmen, who were permitted to cut faggots to sell in Brussels, and 'kohlers,' who made smouldering underground fires, wherewith to convert the tough gnarled roots and stumps of trees into charcoal. And there were also swine-herds and broom-makers, but none were regarded with much favour by the foresters, who suspected, often justly, that these peaceful trades were only a cover for poaching upon their special charge, the deer and wild boars.

So Master Piquard, the under-forester, was by no means pleased when, in a well-sheltered opening under a beautiful spreading beech-tree, he came upon a little woodland hut that he did not remember to have seen before. It was very low and built of sods of turf, but neater than such huts usually were; it was thatched with reeds, had a doorway and a window, the door and shutter both made of reeds set into a frame. The ground had been broken up near the house, and fenced round to protect a few scanty vegetables of the pea and cabbage kind; a pretty white goat with a kid by her side was tethered near; and in front of the door sat a young man with a red cap, a somewhat soldierly-looking beard, and a brown face, busily making a broom with the assistance of a boy and girl of about eleven and twelve years old.

'Ha, fellow! who gave thee leave to sit down here, and slay the Emperor's deer?'

'I'm no slayer of deer!' replied the man. 'I am a broom-maker.'

'You'll not take me in after that sort!' shouted the keeper, offended that no tokens of respect were paid him; 'canst not rise to hear the Emperor's orders?'

Both at once the children here broke in, the boy crying, 'Never heed the brute, Adrian;' the girl, 'Oh sir, don't you see how lame he is. It hurts him to rise!'

Nevertheless Adrian, with one hand on the boy's shoulder, and the other on a crutch-handled staff, struggled to his feet and limped forward, saying with a smile, 'There, sir, you see I am not likely to be a dangerous foe to the Imperial deer.'

There was something in his frank air of equality that angered the forester, who answered roughly, 'Hurt in some poaching brawl.'

'If you list to call it so,' said Adrian, 'since it

K

was verily when the King of France was poaching on the Duke of Savoy's ground in Piedmont. I was then in one of the Walloon regiments under the Marquis of Guasto, and in a fight at a little place called Susa, whereof Meinherr Forester may have heard, I got an arquebus bolt in the knee, which made an end of my wars, alike with men or deer.'

'What proof have you of this?' demanded Piquard, who knew he would not be borne out in any harshness towards a good soldier. Adrian bit his long moustache, but knowing the need of patience, said: 'If the Herr Forester will deign to enter my hut, I will give him what proof he needs beyond the word of an honest man.'

'Here you boy, hold my horse,' roughly called the forester, swinging himself down, and throwing the rein to the boy, then striding over the threshold into the hut, which though only consisting of two chambers, presented an air of homely neatness and comfort which savoured far more of the habits of a Netherlandish boer of the lower class than of those of a squatter in the forest. Over the holy water stoup on one wall was suspended a Crucifix, and near at hand in a kind of trophy, a sword, a long pair of spurs, a brace of pistols, two belts and an arquebus —the equipments, in fact, of a trooper or man-at-arms. Moreover the owner silently produced from a small case attached to the belt, a paper from Captain Vorstander, a well-known leader of his troop, attesting that Adrian Renslaer, of Brussels, a good and true soldier, holding the rank of sergeant, had been discharged on account of being maimed in the knee by a wound at the battle of Susa.

The forester growled and grunted over it, partly from the difficulty he found in reading it, and partly from the desire he felt to discover some flaw in it.

'Sergeant, quotha!' muttered he. 'And pray, what does Master Sergeant if he be an honest man, settled down here in the Emperor's woods, without saying by your leave?'

'What do I? I maintain myself and my young brother and sister by making these brooms, which Pieter sells in Brussels. The Emperor is scarce likely to object to an honest soldier driving an honest trade.'

'Honest indeed, as the cat said when she found the dairy so handy for catching mice,' growled Piquard. 'How am I to let that armoury of yours hang on the walls, in the heart of the Emperor's game?'

'Men don't usually shoot deer with arquebuses in time of peace, even when they have the use of both legs to go after them,' returned Adrian coolly.

'Do you bandy words with me, fellow?' said

Piquard. 'Show me reason good why I should not bring half a dozen prickers to-morrow morning to tear up this hovel of yours and send you and your brooms packing.'

'As you please, Herr Forester,' said Adrian coolly. 'Only whereas I sell my brooms to Captain Vorstander's good hausfrau, and some others, it might come to the Emperor's ears how his old soldiers are treated.'

'His old soldiers! His vile plunderers,' sneered Piquard; but Renslaer's firm front had its effect so far that he added, 'Look you, Herr Sergeant, 'tis not within my duty to leave you all this gunnery. Be you as lame as you show yourself, that boy has a pair of stout legs, and might do no small damage with them.'

'Without powder, eh!' and Adrian's moustache bristled; for he loved his weapons. His arquebus was beautifully carved and inlaid with steel, and his pistols, the spoil of a slain Frenchman, were mounted with silver, but their value only increased Piquard's determination to secure them, and he sharply exclaimed, 'In the Emperor's name! Silence, rogue. Thou mayst think thyself lucky to get off so cheaply. Now, I will leave you here,' he added, after taking down the firearms, 'so long as no injury is done to any living thing belonging to his Highness, boar, deer, hare or coney, pheasant, partridge or quail. The first you touch, woe be to you. Neither may you keep a dog on any pretext.'

'Certainly not,' said Adrian.

'Nor can I have the Emperor's trees and coverts hacked and cut for these brooms of yours. Look you, not a stick is to be touched within yonder dyke, at your peril. There! You hear the terms on which you may remain. And hark! You may send my wife up at St. Hubert's Lodge, a couple of good birch brooms every month by way of fee for my winking at trespassers like you. I shall send a pricker down to fetch away the arquebus. See you have it ready. Soh! boy, can't you hold the horse still? Remember the brooms: the best birch, mind!'

'I'd rather lay it about his back,' cried Pieter passionately, as Master Piquard disappeared among the trees.

'So would I, the rascal!' growled Adrian. 'If I were but as once I was, I should like to see the villain that would so have dared to speak to me.'

'How could you bear it!' cried his little sister, 'to let him take the arquebus Captain Groot gave you, and the pistols you won in single combat?'

''Tis hard enough,' said Adrian, 'but when one is down, one gets the less trampled on if one lies still, my little Gudule; and he was within the letter of his rules. Firearms are not permitted within the forest——'

'And do you mean to send him his brooms?' demanded Pieter, fiercely.

'I don't mean to be swept out of the forest,' answered Adrian.

'You'll not find me carrying them,' returned Pieter, loftily.

'Wait till they are made,' returned Adrian.

'How are they, or any other brooms, to be made if we are not to go within the dyke?' demanded Gudule.

'There's plenty of good stuff outside if you only look for it,' said Adrian.

'No thanks to him,' returned Pieter; 'he has taken our bread away, and expects us to kiss his feet for it, as if he were the blessed Genoveva herself.'

'Well,' said Adrian, 'he *was* more merciful than I expected. I should not have wondered to see our sods flying about our ears, and to find myself hopping off to get a wallet and a dish, wherewith to sit on Church steps! A little more of thy tongue, Piet, and we should have come to that.'

'Never, Adrian. The Saints forefend.'

'Then you must be careful, little ones, both with tongue, and knife, and string, for we live among foes and must be as wary as if we were walking over mines. I have been expecting a visit of this sort ever since we settled down here, and it is very well it is no worse.'

'What? when you lose your arquebus,' sighed Pieter, as Adrian took it down and tenderly rubbed it with a bit of chamois leather. 'Show me once more how you hit the tall Gascon over the stockade!'

'You'll not lose your sword at least, brother,' said Gudule.

'I hope not, but it may be well to put it under my bed, child. Aye and the spurs, lest the pricker should take a fancy to them. We are in their power, and they will have of us what they please. Though, after all, what should it be to me? I shall never wield sword nor wear spurs again!'

'But I may,' cried Pieter proudly.

'Better wield the scales or the ell wand,' said Adrian; 'but Piet, if soldier thou shouldst ever be, or man in authority, bear this hour in mind, and be not hard with them that be at thy mercy. I never was as bad as some of us! I never set fire on peaceful dwelling, nor raised my hand to hurt priest, woman, or child, and yet it comes on me now how the black-eyed Italian mother wailed when we killed her goat, and burnt her mulberry tree for the very gaiety of our hearts, as a bonfire! Ah well! May be the Saints heard her, and sent this ball to disable me, and make me go through what she did.'

A long discordant bray was here heard. It made Pieter start up, and, by Adrian's advice, tie his donkey in the depths of a secluded thicket, lest the pricker should seize him on pretence of respect to the Emperor's woods.

CHAPTER II.

ADRIAN RENSLAER was the son of a linen dealer at Brussels. The family were respectable burghers, not of the great commercial princely degree, but well-to-do in a homely style, and forming part of the democracy of the great guild of linen weavers.

Adrian's father and mother had been swept off early in life by one of the pestilences that so often ravaged mediæval cities, and which caused the wide gap between him and the little brother and sister, who had been spared in consequence of having been put out to nurse at a country farm. Adrian, a big schoolboy, nearly old enough to be apprenticed, came under the care of his grandfather whose second wife did not love the lad, and made home as unpleasant to him as she could. His one comfort was in Vrow Renslaer's own daughter by a former marriage, Doucette Flandrin, a girl about his own age, who rejoiced in having a young companion.

When poor little Pieter and Gudule were brought home, Doucette had done her best to save them from the tyranny of their baby uncle, and the jealousy of her mother. Much she could not do, but she was a good girl who did justice to the education she received from the Béguines, who taught her better things than the lace she made so exquisitely; and she was the one bright spot in Adrian's life.

He was a high-spirited lad, with natural aspirations beyond the loom and ell wand; but these would have been satisfied by sharing in the discipline of the city guard and trained bands if he had found a cheerful kindly welcome at home, or even if he had been allowed to hope for the hand of sweet Doucette in her tight round cap, and formal little white collar.

He was a fair match for her, as indeed her father had been a far poorer man than his own; and for her sake, encouraged by the smile on her dimpled cheek and the welcome in her honest blue eyes, he had endured to be scolded for idleness and all manner of faults whenever he came in, to be ordered about, to live on mere scraps of food, and to see his little brother and sister harshly used. Would not he and Doucette make it all up to them, as soon as his apprenticeship was over, and the rules of the guild permitted him to marry?

His grandfather was growing feeble, and the vrow had shown him reason good not to interfere, so he only durst say a kind word to the children when she was out of hearing. Adrian, at the workshop, had the most of such words, and was secure of his good will. Nay, in the old man's very sight, at the great annual fair, the youth and maiden had exchanged two little silver hearts, and he had looked on and smiled. They were not sixteen, and perhaps he fancied it child's play.

Of course Vrow Renslaer had other views for her daughter, and Doucette was pretty enough to attract glances that excited her ambition. There was a disreputable young man, son to one of the richest burgomasters, who had been spoilt by unlimited supplies from a foolish mother, and by dangling about among the young nobles, incurring their mockery even while they preyed upon him. This youth admired Doucette Flandrin, and her mother, full of hopes and schemes, tried to lure him to her house, and scorned all warnings and entreaties, in the trust to see Doucette one of the richest dames of Brussels.

Everyone save herself knew this to be an utterly delusive hope, and at last the crisis came. Adrian, coming home from practice with the train bands, found Doucette beset by young Dahler. The old servant who accompanied her was incapable of protecting her, and they were in a lonely square in front of a small slightly frequented Church, which Doucette used to visit as that of her patron saint.

Adrian rushed up to the rescue with drawn sword, struck Dahler down, and the two horrified young people saw him lying at their feet, whether dead or alive they knew not; either way the peril to Adrian was great, for the family was powerful. Adrian was only an apprentice, violence in the streets was severely punished, and the evidence of Doucette and her servant was most likely to be set aside.

'Fly!' was reiterated in the ears of the young man alike by the servant, by Doucette, and by the priest who had come out of the Church. 'Fly!' cried Doucette, with streaming eyes, 'I will be faithful! Fly, or it is death!'

Adrian had no other choice, if he would escape prison and probably death. He strove to walk with an indifferent air, though expecting every moment to hear an alarm behind him, and thus at last reached the more frequented streets, where, mingling with the crowd that followed a party of minstrels and jugglers, he had quitted the town, and struck off into the forest.

Among the many little provinces into which the Netherlands were divided, each with its own jurisdiction, it was by no means difficult to escape justice: but so precise were the regulations of trade, that a runaway apprentice was a sort of pariah, and could not hope to find employment in any of the other mercantile cities, which were all closely connected by commercial relations with one another. Indeed a stranger could not enter a city without being closely interrogated at the gates, and it did not take Adrian long to realise that soldiership was his only resource. Fortune favoured him, for he had hardly gained the Roman road which popular tradition ascribed to Queen Brunehault, before he heard the clank of arms and tramp of horses' feet, and was overtaken by a troop of Walloon men-at-arms in the service of Charles V. Tall, strong, and active, and not without military training, the young burgher was a promising recruit, and was accepted with a rough but friendly welcome, and made one of the five attendants who fell to the share of each of those highly equipped horsemen. There was nothing for him to do but to cast in his lot with the band, a fairly respectable one as times went, under a loyal and faithful leader, who kept his engagements, did his best to pay his soldiers, enforce good discipline, and restrain all outrageous violence, except when the fury of his men was both licensed and irresistible. The profession of the mercenary was an evil one at the best, but Adrian was fortunate in his comrades, and saw it on its most honourable and least ferocious side, nor did he lose in it his true, warm, and reverent heart. He wrote twice to his father, but never heard from home during his eight years of service in the wars of Charles V. His courage, and still more his steadiness, intelligence, and education had gradually raised him to the rank of sergeant, a high and responsible one as things then stood, and he had begun to look forward to the possibility of obtaining a command, such as, if Doucette were still free and faithful, would justify him in calling on her to follow his fortunes. It was a wild improbability at that period, but Adrian still cherished the hope, was as loyal to his Doucette as ever noble knight-errant to his only love, and was thereby preserved from incalculable evil. A shattered knee laid him prostrate at Susa in Savoy, and destroyed all future hope. The disabled soldier was merely a blunted instrument, and if he were never likely to be useful again, he was not even worth taking care of. He had to provide for his own expenses, and when defenceless in an enemy's country, his fate must often have been a terrible retribution for all his savage deeds of oppression. Did not three whole French armies absolutely perish in Italy, to say nothing of individual Germans and Spaniards, when every man's hand was against 'the stranger'?

However, Adrian was sufficiently beloved by his comrades, and esteemed by his officers, to secure his personal safety, and even to prevent his being robbed of the heavy belt of coins and the triple gold chain in which the poor fellow had tried to secure his provision for Doucette. There was no preventing them from melting away under the expenses of his long illness and helplessness; and when he could again move about, utterly incapacitated for service, he retained little more than sufficed to secure for him a passage from Nice to Antwerp in a merchant vessel, in which his former captain was likewise going home, to repose upon his laurels as a wealthy householder at Brussels.

Captain Vorstander had an indolent kindness for the promising young soldier, from whom he had expected so much, though he was not inclined to be at any expense or trouble for him. So Adrian had the benefit of the canal boat which carried home the captain, and thence with throbbing heart, leaning on his crutch, went forth in search of the home he had left.

The linen shop bore still the sign of the Purple Lamb he knew of old, but as he stumbled up the steps, it was an unfamiliar voice that asked the browned and bearded soldier what he lacked.

He leant on the front of the stall, trembling as he asked for Meinherr Jacob Renslaer.

'I know of no Renslaer,' was the answer. 'It is Meinherr Bork who holds it now. Any Holland shirting, Herr soldiers; we have it of the best?'

'Not now, friend,' returned Adrian, 'but can you tell me nothing of the family of Renslaer?'

'Not I, sir,' said the man, for people paid an awful respect to soldierly bearing and accoutrements even while they hated them; 'I am serving my wandering year here, and am from Mechlin. Please you, make way; here are fresh bales coming in.'

Two stout porters were bending under heavy loads of linen, and Adrian had to move out of their way, but one grizzled face was familiar to him, and though too well trained in business habits to speak at the moment, he watched them pass, followed to the warehouse, and exclaimed, 'Matthias Matsen!'

'Who calls me?' demanded the porter turning round with a brawny hand to his heated brow, 'a man-at-arms, by St. Gudule! What do you here, sir?'

'I came on the part of a comrade of mine to enquire after Meinherr Renslaer who formerly held the Purple Lamb,' said Adrian.

'Dead these seven years, Heaven rest his soul,' replied the grizzled giant. 'Look you now, sir, these are working hours, and Herr Bork is a sharp man, but if you'll be at my door, a few paces round the corner, just when the convent bell opposite rings out, I'll answer whatever you please about the old folks.'

With this Adrian was forced to be contented. He knew perfectly well old Matthias' den, a sort of open stall or cellar under one of the warehouses; and, not venturing to make himself known nor claim acquaintance with anyone till he could learn the state of affairs, he limped across the place to the nearest Church, where he waited till the working hours were nearly over, and then made his way to the cellar, to which he descended by shallow steps from the street, from which its only light was received. It was under the vault which supported the building, and had a door which could be closed against bad weather. Matthias came hurrying home just as he was making his painful descent, but did not speak till he had seen him safely down, seated him on the only chair, and stirred up the slumbering embers of the fire on the hearth. Then he looked up and said, The young master.'

'Even so,' replied Adrian holding out his hand. 'How goes it with them all, good old friend?'

Matthias' story was given with many a sigh and grunt. He did not exactly know where Doucette was; he believed that she was a serving woman to some Court lady. Pieter and Gudule were at Tirlemont with their stepmother, who had married a third time, and the little half-brother was dead. That was what Adrian first discovered. Next he heard that Dahler had not been killed by his blow, but had been severely injured, and that he and his father had shown a bitter spirit of hatred and revenge against all the Renslaer family, insisting on their producing the culprit, and then doing their utmost to ruin their trade and hunt them down. Old Renslaer soon died, and on his death his affairs were found to be in a state of hopeless confusion. Dahler's spite had hindered his grandchildren from being adopted by the guild to which the old man had belonged, and his widow had taken them away with her to Tirlemont, whence she had originally come. That was all the old man knew, except that Doucette had kept all suitors at bay by declaring a previous contract with Adrian, sanctioned by his grandfather and her stepfather; and he had actually seen her, within the last year, come to the shop to purchase a fine web of linen for some great Countess or Duchess in whose service she was.

He made Adrian welcome with all his heart to his supper and his bed, but told him that the Dahlers were a vindictive race, and both for his blow and his flight he might be called to account.

Adrian slept in the cellar that night, then made his way with great perseverance, but terrible pain and toil to Tirlemont, leaving his weapons with Matthias, and spending on the way nearly his last few coins, coming into the place with a troop of market people, one of whom had good-naturedly given the lame soldier a ride in a cart. He decided on sitting for a time on some steps that overlooked the market-place, both to rest and to observe, since he was nearly certain that the market would afford a full muster of the women of Tirlemont.

In truth it did so, and Adrian had no difficulty in recognising the portly form and ill-tempered face of his grandfather's wife, as she marched in with her wide flapping cap and the bunch of keys at her girdle. There were no signs of poverty about her, but she was followed by two almost ragged, half-starved little children, carrying a basket between them. Adrian's teeth were set, and his hand grasped the hilt of his dagger in his rage at the sight of the load of heavy roots and fruits under which the poor little things staggered away behind her, so slowly perforce, in spite of her scolding, that he had no difficulty in keeping them in sight till they disappeared in an open doorway. By making enquiries in the street he learnt that Vrow Renslaer had joined a sister of hers, and that together they took in the washing of various citizen families, and the getting up of the delicate Flemish ruffs and cuffs that make such a figure at the time. His informant, a burly Franciscan friar, added with a shrug that it was a hard and ungodly house, and that he pitied the two poor children. Vrow Renslaer, it seemed, excused herself from all charitable contributions on the ground of being saddled with her husband's orphan grandchildren; and 'the Saints help them,' said the gossiping friar, 'the poor things are worked harder than any galley slave at Tangier!'

On this Adrian ventured to communicate to the good-natured friar who he was, and to consult him how to find means of speaking to his brother. The little mystery delighted Brother Andreas, who laboured under the misfortune of having far too little to do, and he undertook to invent an errand which should bring Pieter out without loss of time.

Upsetting his wallet on the ground, he waddled hastily into the door, exclaiming, 'Vrow, dear Vrow, I ask no bounty to-day, but lend me Pieter; my wallet is fallen! All the alms of the faithful are in the dirt, and how am I to get them to the house without help? Here, Pieter—Ah! the good boy is already gone——'

He was gone, without waiting to hear the Vrow's scoldings and charges to him not to idle on the way; but she had her irons hot, and could not stir to pursue or look after him.

Sooth to say, Brother Andreas did not concern himself much about his quest, and the whole contents of the wallet were one sausage and half a loaf; but the boy was already in the arms of his brother, and had come to the knowledge that the battered, bearded, crippled soldier was really Adrian. The cunning friar hastily filled his wallet with stones, and taking one corner, while Pieter took the other, the trio slowly proceeded towards the convent. Pieter had full time to tell his tale. Doucette, he said, had stood by them, and shielded them as much as possible, but he verily believed Vrow Renslaer would have turned them out to beg, if Doucette had not taken service with the young Countess d'Espinay, one of the Empress' ladies, and promised to send all the money she earned in wages for their maintenance. 'We had rather beg than live as we do,' said poor little Pieter, 'but Doucette always begged us to bear it, lest you should not be able to find us when you came home! O Adrian, I looked to see you come on horseback with a hat and feather.'

A terrible account of blows, overwork, and starvation was elicited from the boy; and he implored Adrian to take them away.

It was early summer, and life in the woods looked fresh and fair. Adrian thought at first of openly demanding his brother and sister from the Vrow; but the friar dissuaded him, lest she should denounce him to the authorities at Brussels, and Pieter and Gudule were therefore to watch their opportunity run away, and meet their brother at the Church of the convent. There Friar Andreas promised the soldier a meal and a night's lodging in case of need, and in fact the time Pieter resolved on was early morning, when he and his sister were sure to be sent to take home the linen for the Sunday wear of the neighbouring burgomaster.

Trembling and panting, but supremely happy, poor little Gudule, a mere skeleton dressed in threadbare rags, darted into Adrian's arms. Just as the first Mass was over at five o'clock in the morning Brother Andreas, almost as much delighted as the children, gave them their breakfast, and borrowed for Adrian's use the donkey which accompanied the brethren on their more distant quests, coming with them himself for the earlier part of their journey, which he directed with the sagacity of one well used to roaming the country.

He was a kind and honest man, though not by any means of a high tone, and with him, ways and means were discussed. Every trade was so close a corporation that the runaway apprentice and disabled soldier had no chance of employment; no city accepted strangers except in the most menial situations; and besides Adrian, after the free open air life of the camp, knew not how to brook confinement in one of the horrible dens to which city life in such a capacity would have condemned him.

The accident of meeting an ass loaded with brooms decided him. He knew he could make them, for he had had in the beginning of his warlike career a Dutch man-at-arms, who had forced his grooms to sweep his tent and their own stables into tidiness like the village of Brock, and had even been critical about the brooms they made for the purpose. He remembered too that there had been a scarcity of the article at Brussels, for the Vrow's shrill murmurs at the cost of besoms still rang in his ears. So he resolved that, for the summer at least, he would take shelter in the outskirts of the wood of Soignies, near enough to Brussels to send Pieter in to dispose of them, when old Matthias would be able to give him advice and patronage; near Brussels too it was just possible that something might be heard of Doucette, whose mistress was one of the ladies of the Empress Isabel. Poor Adrian knew himself to have sunk far beneath her level in society, but he knew her to be still unwedded and to be still holding to her contract, and thus hope was not dead. His lameness might diminish enough to enable him to obtain some better employment. In short, hope can with difficulty be killed when a man has lived but a quarter of a century.

Thus it was that the brothers and their little sister made their way to the outskirts of Soignies on the Brussels side, where game was not so thick as to lead many huntsmen that way, and there was plenty of material for their trade. A soldier like Adrian was experienced in the resources of the bivouac, and devised shelter for Gudule under branches of trees till the hut could be built. Pieter was sent in to tell Matthias Matsen, and under his supervision to sell some of Adrian's more costly accoutrements and lay out the sum on a few necessaries of life, which the stout porter carried out to them on the first holy day. Holy days came thickly in early May, and Matthias had no scruple in devoting all their later hours, and those of the Sundays, to the raising of Master Adrian's roof-tree, and the general comfort of the little settlement.

It was he too that showed Pieter where to carry his brooms, and who spoke words of recommendation that made the trade flourish. The children had never been so happy in their lives. Gudule could not remember a time when she had not been cowed and misused, and it was like Paradise to have to live a full life with an indulgent brother instead of being scolded, driven, and kept to hard toil all day long.

All play had long been driven out of her, and she was a solemn little housewifely Fleming; but she knew how to fulfil all sorts of household tasks, and the blissful change was to do them for love, be thanked, praised and wondered at, then to hear the birds sing, listen to Adrian's stories of strange lands; and neither be beaten herself nor see Pieter beaten.

Thus the summer months were passing with very fair prosperity, and much enjoyment to the children, who were growing plump and strong; and Pieter's trade had become fairly established when Master Piquard's visit filled them with uneasiness.

CHAPTER III.

THE pricker did not fail to come the next morning to take away the firearms; but he turned out to be an old soldier, who had fought in Maximilian's Italian campaigns, and was pleased to find someone who could talk about Lombardy, and join with him in vituperation of landsknechts, Swiss, and all in fact who were not Netherlanders. He sympathised with Adrian on the loss of his weapons, but observed that it had been a mere folly to keep them when they might have been turned into good guilders for their owner instead of for Master Piquard. However, he liked Adrian the better for clinging to them, and, so far from making any further perquisitions, told him that if anyone below the degree of the forester Piquard annoyed him, he might appeal to the protection of himself, Hans Rink.

This protection stood them in good stead, otherwise they could hardly have held their ground against Piquard's petty persecutions. Pieter had to go farther for his material, and to bring home what was not available without double the amount of sorting and picking, and he often grumbled heartily, if he did not sometimes transgress. He had fewer brooms to take to Brussels, and not only did Piquard make him pay toll on them, but the under-prickers and their boys used to hoot at him, and drive him away when he was within bounds. There were outlaws haunting the forest, who expected Adrian to make common cause with them, and when they found him too true to his training both as citizen and soldier, began to hold him in sufficient distrust and dislike to make him heartily regret the loss of his arquebus.

One morning Gudule, going into the wood to gather berries, found a poor little fawn running round and vainly caressing its dead mother, who, poor thing, must have fled pierced by an outlaw's arrow, only to die.

Gudule caught the poor little creature with some difficulty, brought it home, and with much patience and tenderness managed to make it drink some goat's milk and water. She was so happy with it, that Adrian, though he thought it a perilous possession, could not bear to deprive her of it, but by way of precaution, he sent Picter to Hans Rink to report on the discovery.

Rink was not at home, and Pieter most unwillingly was forced to follow him to Piquard's lodge. There was a terrible baying of hounds, which almost daunted the boy's heart, as the dogs stood at the length of their chains, leaping and growling at him, and the forester and prickers, coming forth at the sound, to laugh at the alarm of the boy, and to shout at them till they sprang at their chains half maddened.

Rink, however, no sooner recognised the boy than he came forward, took him by the hand, and led him up to tell his business, whereat Piquard laughed with a sneer, but sent down two prickers to secure the venison. Pieter tried to guide them to the spot, but either the doe was gone, or else he missed the spot, though he called Gudule to help him. Round and round the ash-tree she remembered did they wander in vain, and even the two prickers laughed at Adrian for being too dull or too scrupulous to have helped himself to it. Indeed one at least believed that he had done so, and had only sent Pieter with the information as a blind—nay, Piquard's reading of the matter was that one or other of the brothers had been the slaughterer of the deer. He was sure Renslaer was not as lame as he pretended. In truth, Adrian was less lame than when he had arrived, and could stand and walk much longer; his health was recovering itself, and if he had ventured to make his hut more solid and comfortable, or do anything to attract the notice and suspicion of his petty tyrant, his situation would have been very comfortable.

Looking forward, however, to the winter, when the paths would be blocked with snow, and the keen winds would blow through the frail hut, he doubted whether Gudule could safely remain through the inclement season, and whether, indeed, all three might not perish with cold and hunger, if they did not find lodging in some town or village. For this he strove to save; but the daily needs were absorbing all the profits of the trade, and the immediate expectation of the Court at Brussels made the foresters all the more alert.

'You, Renslaer, here!' shouted Piquard, very splendid in a new hunting suit of green. 'The Emperor is come to Brussels. There's to be no cutting of so much as a sprig of heather or spray of birch while he is here.'

'That is just starvation,' said Adrian.

'What care I whether beggars starve or not? I have left you here too long, to steal the Emperor's deer, and take his eggs; but I'm too good-natured, and shall have to answer for it if he finds this trespassing hut.'

'It is beyond the bounds——'

'Do you bandy words with me, you plunderer? I give you a week to be off, and then down comes this house.'

Whether this was meant in earnest or as a means of extortion, Adrian knew not, for Piquard gallopped away, while Gudule stood weeping, sobbing, and clinging to her brother.

Pieter was sent that evening to consult Hans Rink, but again could not find him. However, late in the evening, the old man came down with a big basket over his shoulder.

'Here!' he said; 'there's been a mighty chase, and the great folk have killed more than they listed to carry away, so I brought down a breast and shoulder for the little maid to try her skill on.'

'O dear good Hans, thanks; but hast thou heard what Master Piquard swears,' she anxiously answered. 'That he gives us but a week, and then he will pull down the hut over our heads?'

'Piquard swears to do more than he doth,' said Adrian.

'That is true, and for my part, were I you, I would wait till the worst came. You could but be off then. The whole of us will be far too busy attending on the Emperor for the pulling down of huts; and it might even be, if the chase came this way, you might get a word to the Emperor himself. He is a kindly man to speak to, they say, and loves an old soldier and a Fleming. They tell me he is never so much at home, nor so merry, in all his lands, as here in good old Brabant. No, no! Herr Serjeant, stick to your hut as long as you can, and call St. Hubert to aid, for I believe you are a lucky man, and will get off this time. Keep your fawn and your goat close, little maid, or the dogs may be on them, and bring you into trouble. And for you young Pieter, you come with me, and I'll show you a bundle of heather you can carry off, that will serve you for a week's work. No, no! Serjeant, no thanks. I was a soldier before I was a pricker, and we of the Walloons always stand by one another.'

'At least you will come and see how Gudule deals with your venison?'

'That must be as the hunters will it! I can't tell where I may be, at this end of the forest or far away by Ardennes, after the boars. But be cautious, and good St. Hubert have you in his keeping!'

CHAPTER IV.

Sounds of the chase, the winded horn and the baying of the dogs, had been fitfully heard, now near, now farther off, all day, but as the twilight of a September evening fell, they died away in the distance. Then it was that Gudule went out with her pitcher to the spring to fetch water for the evening meal. As she stood holding it to catch the drops that oozed from a high bank and were collected by a hollow tile before falling into the pool below, she caught the sound of a horse's feet on the short turf behind her, and dreading Master Piquard, was snatching back her pitcher, and taking the first bound for her intended flight, when a voice of far different tone called, 'Ho là, my little maiden.'

She paused and saw, coming through the bushes, the figure of a man, leading a weary stumbling horse, with its head hanging down.

'You have water there, maiden,' he said. 'Can my horse drink?'

'Here is a pool, sir,' said Gudule, half frightened,

half reassured, as the stranger led his white horse forward, and removed the bit, so that it might drink freely. Gudule shyly held out her pitcher to the man himself, and he said, 'Thanks, dear little one,' in a more courtly and gentle tone than she had ever heard, took the earthenware pitcher, drained it, with his head thrown back, and restored it with renewed thanks, for 'as welcome a draught as ever I tasted. And now, little maid,' he added, 'canst thou tell a wearied hungry hunter where to find rest and food for himself and his horse, and then guidance out of this forest where I have lost my way?'

'My brothers live near at hand, sir,' replied Gudule, quite reassured by the gentleness of the voice, and fearlessly leading the way to the hut, where the firelight gleamed through the open door.

Adrian and Pieter both started up at the sound of horses' hoofs, and Gudule darted forward. 'O brother, he is a lost hunter! and his poor horse is so weary—may I not bring him in?'

'I will reward you well, dear sirs,' said the hunter, in a voice that did indeed show weariness and exhaustion. 'A mouthful of food for myself and my steed, an hour's rest, and a guide to set me on my way, is all I ask.'

'You are welcome, sir,' replied Adrian. 'Come in, and sit down. At least we can give you shelter, and a share of our supper, rude though it be,' he added apologetically, for as the stranger came forward into the light, his bearing as well as his voice showed him to be of gentle blood.

'Thanks, comrade,' was his reply. 'A soldier knows how to be thankful for a roof and a crust; and you are a soldier,' he added, recognising Adrian's military salute.

'I have served, sir,' replied Adrian shortly.

'Then you know that a man's horse is his first care. Can you bestow my poor Ali safely for me, and give him a feed? There is a storm coming up, and I would not leave him outside.'

'He deserves care,' said Adrian, taking the bridle. 'Why! this is a true barb, such as I have seldom seen save belonging to Spanish Dons!' continued he, as he fastened the horse to a hook in the wall of the cottage, bade Pieter bring in a bundle of the hay stored for the goat and donkey, and with ' by your leave, sir,' began to rub down the tired animal in true groom-fashion. He could not help doing so for love and pity for the beautiful Barbary horse, guessing that the horse's master, however willing, might not be able to perform these services, for in these degenerate days, pages and squires left such occupations to grooms and horseboys instead of deeming them part of noble training. His guest thanked him heartily, looked on with great satisfaction, and sat down on a low bench by the fire, where Gudule was stirring up her *pot au feu*. His dress was the plainest possible green hunting suit, with a sheathed knife stuck in the belt, and a low-crowned, narrow-brimmed hat, such as was worn in Flanders. When the flame played on his features, the face was that of a man of about forty years old, with a light-coloured beard and hair inclining to red, a pale complexion, a peculiar long heavy chin and underlip, and keen blue eyes that seemed to each person in the room to be fixed on him or her, observing every movement. His speech was the native Flemish, very quiet, gentle, and courteous; but he was plainly exceedingly weary, and was grateful when on a whisper from Gudule, Pieter fetched some slippers that Adrian had brought home, and offered to pull off his heavy boots.

'Thanks,' said the guest. 'This is comfort I expected not.'

'I brought them from Nizza,' said Adrian, rather ashamed of the luxury. 'My wound was my excuse. It was long before I could wear aught else.'

'You were in Piedmont then. Where were you hurt?'

Adrian answered, and various military recollections were discussed, while Adrian completed the grooming of the horse, and Gudule, fetching from some recess a big earthenware dish, one wooden bowl, and three horn spoons, proceeded to lift her caldron from over the fire and pour the contents into the dish on the table. She had the pie made of Rink's venison safe in her larder (the bottom of an old cask), but that was kept in reserve to be used in case, according to his threat, Piquard cut off the supplies. And Gudule's *pot au feu* was considered as almost dainty, though it was little but a stew of barley broth thickened with meal, flavoured with earth nuts, sorrel, and such woodland vegetables as Flemish thrift employed; and as the present brew was enriched by all the scraps of meat, fat and bones which had not gone into the pasty, Gudule viewed it with pride as a dish fit to set before a king.

She put some barley cakes by each dish, observed that all was ready, and took up her pitcher to fetch some more water, but a heavy storm of rain drove her back.

'We wait for the hostess,' said the guest.

'That is noble fashion, not burgher fashion,' said Adrian. 'Gudule had rather sup after us, so please you, sir.'

The sign of the Cross was made, the Benedicite said, and for the first few mouthfuls from the bowl the stranger seemed only conscious of the satisfaction of the warmth, then he slackened a little, and as a slight sound outside caused Gudule to open the door and admit her fawn, he noticed it and held out his hand with a bit of bread. The creature with a frightened eye, hid itself behind its mistress, and Adrian knowing it was dangerous possession, explained how his little sister had found it by its dead mother, and they had not the heart to turn it away to starve.

'Ay, ay,' said the guest, 'the bravest soldier, the softest heart. So say the English, and I would that our warriors would take the lesson from them.'

'The Emperor taught them so far,' said Adrian, 'when he would not have his tent struck because the swallows had there made their nest.'

'Ah, ha! thou wast there, friend,' said the guest. 'You and your Walloons stood us in good stead. By my faith, the Frenchman came on like a thunder cloud.'

'True, sir, but as an old captain said—Once stand firm and break the Frenchmen, and they will dash themselves to pieces for very spite.'

'Was that old Groot? a stout old Dutchman, a very stone wall for the *furia Francese* to launch against?'

So the two soldiers talked; but on arriving at the bottom of his bowl, the stranger, now quite at home, paused and said, 'Excellent broth, my good little maid; methinks it hath a flavour of the late parent of yonder favourite of thine. You who live in these woods have your opportunities, and I trow those skilful hands find exercise on something better than barley broth.'

'We never touch the Emperor's deer,' said Adrian. 'I know my orders too well for that; but one of the prickers, an old soldier, hath at times brought us portions of his share.'

'So I guessed,' said the visitor drily;'' but never fear, I'm not the man to betray the secrets of a kindly host and comrade in the wars. Ah, ah! I thought as much,' as Gudule, at a sign from her brother, and with thorough good will, produced the pasty of her pride, into the depths of which he forthwith plunged, devouring at a rate, which might be complimentary to her cookery, but which made her heart quail at the thought of her week's provision, and Pieter sigh at the rapid vanishing of so rare a dainty.

Of drink there was nothing to be had but a horrible brew which Gudule had attempted to make with wild fruits, and which all her guest's courtesy could not induce him to swallow. He accepted a draught of goat's milk and water, over which he sat talking in a friendly manner with Adrian over the campaigns in Provence and at Tunis, in which both had been concerned, and obtaining the Fleming's whole story, though he was not himself equally communicative. All he said of himself was that he came from Ghent, and had been a good many years at Court; he had gone out with the Imperial hunt that day, and had lost himself in the forest, and taken a wrong turn after the killing of a great wild boar. He wished the beast's collops were there for his kind little hostess to fry. Could he do nothing for his good friends, in case he had speech of the Emperor?

'O yes,' cried Pieter, 'to get leave for us to cut wood and heather for our brooms where we will, in spite of Piquard!'

'To hinder Piquard from driving us out of house and home,' added Gudule.

'Mayhap my interest may go so far,' said the guest; 'but even if so much were granted, you could hardly spend a winter here.'

'I thought once we could have weathered it through,' said Adrian, 'had we leave to cut wood to make the house weather-tight, and means enough to lay in a stock of salt meat and fish to serve us when the way to the town is blocked; but since the forester has set himself against us, our trade has lessened, and we have naught beforehand.'

''Tis a hard life for a little maiden and a crippled man,' said the stranger thoughtfully.

'We did well in the summer,' said Adrian, 'and for the winter we must bide Heaven's will, either nesting here, or taking shelter in town or village. I'm loth to go into Brussels, for let a man have served ever so many years, our burghers can't forget that he is but a runaway apprentice; and Dahler might any day bring me to my trial, or throw me into prison, which would be worse.'

No more was said that night, for the stranger applied himself to the telling of his beads. He would not have a bed given up to him, but wrapped himself in a horseman's cloak that was rolled up in front of his saddle, and lay down before the fire.

Probably he was used to an easier couch, for before it was light, he was on foot, spending a long time on his knees before the Crucifix and asking where his hosts heard Mass. Pieter and Gudule used to go to Mont St. Jean on Sunday, but it was too far off for Adrian as yet, though he had improved so much that he hoped to be able to hear Mass on All Saints Day. The stranger gave up the notion of going to Mass when he heard the distance, and after fortifying himself with another large wedge of pie, requested Pieter to put him on the road back into Brussels.

Out they went, just as morning sunshine was beginning to touch the tops of the trees, and to sparkle in the drops left by the storm of the previous evening. Adrian had saddled the horse, and stood holding the bridle. There was a soldierly erectness about his figure, and a satisfaction in handling a good horse, which were not lost on his guest, who said, 'Warm thanks, friend; the Walloons have lost a good soldier, and Brussels a good citizen in thee. Would that something could be done for thee! Fare thee well, my little housewife! I wish thee plenty of pasties to make and better berries to brew.' And away he rode, with as courtly a wave of his hat to little Gudule as though she had been a young baroness in a balcony.

'I would he had come when that pasty had been further off,' sighed Adrian.

'He has eaten it almost all up,' said Gudule disconsolately. 'What shall we say to Master Rink?'

'Psha! that is not what I am thinking of!'

'He would never betray us, brother!'

'I would I knew that! Those court gentlemen are mad where game is concerned, and a court gentleman he is, and half a Spaniard too; I knew it by his hands, and by the air with which he flung on his cloak. None but the Don has that trick; and once in their hands, all is at an end with you. They know not what mercy means, and they are bitterly jealous of us Flemings because the Emperor loves us best, Heaven preserve him!'

'The Emperor is half Spanish too,' said Gudule.

'More's the pity, but he is a Fleming born, a man of Ghent like this gentleman.'

'A gentleman, Adrian? He had not even a gold chain!'

'Child, canst not tell a gentleman but by the gold chain?'

'If gentleman he be,' said the little housewife, bustling about to put things away, 'I hope he may pay Pieter well, for he has eaten enough of our pasty to last the whole three of us for two days!'

CHAPTER V.

PIETER came home, holding by the edge a big silver coin, new and bright, with a scalloped edge, and stamped with two shields, crowned, and flanked by two columns, *i.e.*, the pillars of Hercules, with the proud legend '*Plus ultra.*' A Spanish doubloon it was without doubt, and in spite of Adrian's detestation of things Spanish, he was very glad to welcome it, and took it as a proof of the high quality of the bewildered huntsman, for the worth was nominally about nine shillings of our money, an enormous sum for a bed and supper, even to a man of such voracious appetite.

Pieter said he had acted as guide as far as a convent in the suburbs of Brussels, where the gentleman had gone in to hear Mass, giving his horse to the porter, and rewarding Pieter with this piece of silver. The boy had gone with him into the Church, but had lost sight of him there.

Far as he had walked, the boy was ready to set out again to take the coin to Matthias to be changed, but Gudule wanted to keep it to look at, or to wear on Sundays as a medal round her neck, and Adrian thought that it ought to be kept in reserve against times of trouble; so Pieter had to return to the cutting of heather, and revolve in his mind all the purchases that could be made with this great wealth; while Gudule sat down to her spinning.

The day did not, however, pass without a great shock. One of the men-at-arms of the Emperor's own guard rode up on a large black horse, and in much mispronounced Flemish, said, 'Adrian Renslaer, you are summoned to appear before the Ducal Chamber.'

Adrian, in no small consternation, demanded why; but the emissary, a Spaniard, could or would understand nothing but pure Castillian, and turned a deaf ear to the *lingua franca* that Adrian had acquired as a soldier. He pointed to a rough cart that had lumbered up behind him, and made it plain that he would brook no delay. Adrian could hardly take the certificate of his services from his belt, muttering to himself and to the sobbing weeping children, "Betrayed, denounced! I ought not to have trusted the Spanish blood. A plague upon the venison! Look you, Pieter, it will be of no use, they will swear away my life: or what amounts to the same, my good right hand. But as a last hope, go thou to seek out Hans

Rink, and bring him to bear testimony as to that venison. Yet he too may have aided in baiting the trap.'

Picter's attempt to set forth was, however, frustrated by the Spaniard, who laid a heavy hand on him and said, '*Los niños van.*' With sinking hearts, then, all were bestowed in the cart, which was led by a dull heavy boor to whom their escort would not permit them to speak.

Gudule sat sobbing and moaning to herself, 'If I had but guessed! Oh the viper! Who would have thought it when he spoke so kindly?'

Adrian remained silent with his face hidden on his knees till the wood was nearly passed, and then he looked up, and said, 'Children, if the worst betide me, and I go to prison or to death without seeing you more, you had best go to old Matthias. He will give you shelter for a night or two. Mayhap then, one of the good Béguines would concern herself about Gudule and find a place as a servant-wench for her. It would be a hard life, but not so hard as going back to the Vrow grandmother; and the good sister Ursula, who bred up Doucette, would seek thee a good home, my poor little one. For thee, Picter, Matthias might find a service, or Captain Groot would say a good word for thee in my old troop, where there are many that would befriend a Renslaer.'

Poor little Gudule wept and sobbed so much that she hardly gathered the sense of his words, but Pieter looked up in his face without a word, only nodding his head to intimate that he heard.

'And,' concluded Adrian, in a lower tone, 'if ever either one of you should ever meet her again, let her know that I have been faithful to the last, and that the little heart she wots of will go with me to the end. And so the good God and the Saints have you in keeping!'

Through the gates, through the familiar streets, meeting many wondering but few pitying eyes, went the melancholy cartload, even to the gateway of the grand old ducal palace, inhabited at present by the Court, with the many quartered banner of the Emperor floating high above it. The word was given and they entered the gates, and were halted in the outer courtyard, where they were ordered to descend from the cart, and conducted into an inner quadrangle, belonging to the household itself, and surrounded by long balconies or galleries communicating with one another by outside staircases. Here the guards stopped their prisoners, while a message was sent into the interior of the palace. Then it was that Gudule, looking up to gaze drearily, yet not incuriously round through her tears, saw a trimly dressed young serving woman, in stiff white cap, neat dark stuff gown, and

gaily trimmed apron, looking pitifully over the richly
pieced stone balustrade at their mournful group. Their
eyes met, and in another moment, with a little cry,
the girl had sprung down the stairs and was beside
them. 'Gudule! Pieter!' she said. 'How are you
here? What trouble is this?'

'Ah! Doucette! my heart is light,' cried Adrian,
with a start of joy that altered his whole face and
person. 'Now I fear nothing. I have seen thee.'

'Thou! oh! my poor Adrian, is it thus?'

'Mistress Doucette, what do you? Fie! lingering
thus in the court with the men folk!' cried a sharp
voice from above. 'The Countess shall hear of this!'

'He is my betrothed! I have found him!' was
Doucette's cry.

'A prisoner! evil girl! under guard. Come away
instantly.'

'Were he ten times a prisoner he is my betrothed,'
exclaimed the girl. 'Oh Adrian! why art thou thus?
what hast thou done?'

But Adrian had not had time to answer before
the summons came, 'Lead him into the hall.' He
could only mutter, 'Naught—it is a trap,' before he was
hurried on, as fast as his stiff limb would permit,
leaning on his brother; but the crowd closed in and
Gudule was left crying in Doucette's arms.

Meantime Adrian and Pieter were led into the

hall. It was full of people—soldiers, yeomen, citizens, crowds of all sorts standing below, having been admitted to see the Emperor dine. Above, there were ranks of the most splendid chivalry in Europe—Spanish, Italian, Flemish, Dutch, German, in their graceful sixteenth century costume, preserving a touch of nationality in dress, besides the Golden Fleece round some necks, and the Cross of Santiago round others.

The centre of all this splendour was a table, laid for one. The meal was over, but tall Venice flasks and silver glasses were on the board, with walnuts and apples. Two jesters in cap and bells stood behind a chair of state, in which was seated a figure in black velvet, the Golden Fleece round his neck, beneath his rufous beard.

Adrian dropped, as well as he could, on his sound knee, Pieter on both. A hearty laugh, in a not unfamiliar tone, greeted them. 'Ho! ho, my good comrade! I owe you a supper! Where is your little housewife and capital cook?'

'She is here, Sire,' said Adrian, looking up so much startled at missing her that he forgot all else.

'Fetch her in,' said the Emperor. 'You, Pieter, go with that good fellow, who knows you.'

Then Adrian saw that Rink and Piquard, as well as Captain Vorstander, were all standing not far off.

'Yes,' said Charles, 'my good gossips here would

have given me no peace had I not looked into your story, though I knew better than to distrust the word of an honest Brabanter.

'Ha, here comes our little pie-maker, and on my word, another damsel with her. What's this? Another sister?'

'No, Sire,' said Doucette, coming forward with a boldness that electrified all present, 'I am his betrothed; I have not seen him since he was forced to flee because of the blow he struck in my defence nine years ago, but he is mine, and I am his, and I claim to share his lot;' and she took his hand.

The two jesters, as was their cue, muttered something about surpassing fools, and the Emperor, putting on a grim face, said: 'Share it thou shalt, maiden. Art thou ready for prison, or for exile? Knowest thou the penalty of eating our ducal deer?'

'No hand to give thee,' put in one of the jesters, as Doucette looked up scared.

'Then will I work for him,' said she, with a face so full of dauntless love and bitter grief that none there could ever forget it.

'Give her to me, friend Charles,' cried the jester; 'she's a hopeless fool.'

'Here,' said Charles, holding out a paper—'Here is thy sentence, bold broom maker. Canst read it aloud?'

Adrian, as a soldier well used to obeying orders, made his salute, took the paper, and read aloud:—

'We, Charles, by the grace of God King of Germany, of the Romans, Italy and Lombardy, King of Castille and Arragon, of the two Sicilies and Jerusalem, Archduke of Austria, Duke of Brabant, and Count of Holland, Zealand and Friesland, hereby give and grant unto trusty Adrian Renslaer, late serjeant in the Walloon infantry, two hundred acres of land in the parish of St. Jean, in the wood of Soignies, to be held by him and his heirs for ever, with licence to graze his cattle and cut birch and heather within our forest of Soignies, on the tenure of the delivery of a broom to our chamberlain at our palace at Brussels, on the feast of St. Matthew, yearly by him and his heirs for ever. Given at our palace at Brussels this feast of St. Matthew in the year of grace 1540.

'I the King.'

Adrian could but kiss the hand the Emperor held out.

'Will that do, kind host, and little maid?' said the Emperor. 'It seemed to me better than trying to set matters straight with these fellow-burghers of thine, who stickle for privileges even against their lawful Duke.'

'Verily, Sire,' said Adrian, 'I love to hear the merle sing better than the mouse squeak.'

'I thought as much,' said Charles. 'Now, my steward shall do his best to repay thy hospitality in kind, and thou, little maiden, shalt see whether our pasties equal thine. Come hither, my guide,' he added; 'I have an order for thee;' and as the wondering Pieter obeyed, he said, 'I give thee a fortnight. On this day fortnight bring as many brooms as ye all can make, and stand at the corner of St. Gudule's Church. So fare ye all well.'

They were dismissed, but were led off by crowds congratulating them. Even Piquard begged them to remember that he had always stood their friend! The Count d'Espinay, who had recognised his wife's serving woman, came to them as they crossed the hall, and bade Doucette take Gudule to her lady, who, like everyone else, was burning with curiosity to understand the story of the Emperor's pleasantry.

The difficulty remained, how the farm was to be stocked or the house built. Adrian's means amounted to little more than the doubloon given to Pieter, and Doucette's fees, small enough in themselves, had all been sent to her mother for the support of the children, whom she had supposed still to be at Tirlemont. They must still work, and she must continue in service and save. So agreed the patient Flemish spirits, grateful that the long severance of these nine years was over; and Adrian went back with the children to the hut, where all fear and peril had ceased, to fulfil the Emperor's behest as to the brooms.

Heartily they worked, and Rink came to aid them whenever he could. He even brought two donkeys on the appointed morning to carry in the brooms, with which in due time Pieter took his stand close beneath the steps of beautiful St. Gudule's Church.

His first customer was a dainty languid-looking Italian, with disdainful eyes. '*Una—come si dice? una scopa, un balai, mio ragazzo.*'

By the gesture rather than the words, Pieter understood, and held out a broom. A great silver coin was in his hand; he looked about for change, and tried to say it was far too much; but the Italian was dreamily dragging his birch behind him, and as the boy was about to run after him, a stout Dutch ecclesiastic arrested him. 'How now, knave, don't be off when I want thy wares, thy brooms.'

'He has paid me over-much,' said Pieter, panting. 'Look here, holy sir, what is this?'

'A ducat: over much, yea; but don't trouble thyself, boy, 'tis a whim we all have to follow. Give me a besom, I say. There! Thou'lt not get the like another day.'

It was a piece not equal to a ducat, but far beyond

the value of the broom. The astonished Pieter had no time to remonstrate, for a German baron came growling and strutting up, and gave him so small a coin that he doubted whether it were even the full value of his broom; but to make up for that, two exceedingly splendid young Flemish knights strolled laughing towards him, each seized on a broom, threw down a gold piece, and walked off sparring at each other with the broom-sticks. Then followed a lean, shrewd, much disgusted, black-gowned, square-capped lawyer-statesman, who laid hold of his broom-handle, scarcely looking at it, threw down its exact market price, and hurried away with it over his shoulder, only pausing at the instance of an exceedingly haughty Spanish grandee, with drooping hat and feather, and mantle over one shoulder, who was evidently asking him if it were necessary to saddle himself with so degrading a badge, but being assured that it was, twirled up his moustaches, stalked forward, and in a voice far gentler than his appearance, said, ' *Una escoba, mi niño,*' handing over another of those beautiful doubloons, and shaking his head when Pieter proffered change. Then came Doucette's master, the Count d'Espinay, and with him a tall beautiful lad of eighteen with long brown curled hair and bright soft brown eyes.

'How goes it, my little fellow,' demanded Espinay; 'are you winning a fortune for your brother?'

'It is marvellous, my lord; they snatch them from me, and will stay for no change, and I always was a honest lad and dealt fairly,' said poor Pieter much distressed.

'He has not found it out,' said the younger man. 'What! knowest thou not the Emperor's trick for making thy fortune? He has issued an order that not a man shall be admitted to his reception without carrying a broom! Here they come, half a dozen more of them! How many more brooms hast thou? Only a dozen and a half? Oh! this will never do! This is a full court day, and there are at least two hundred more who have to come. Monsieur d'Espinay, lend me your purse. Keep them in play, little man, till I return.'

'Be prudent, my dear Lamoral,' began the Count d'Espinay. But the youth was already gone, and just as Pieter's stock was waxing low, back he came with two stout porters bending under piles of brooms, and followed by two more with barrows full. Moreover he stood by Pieter, and assisted in the sale, with all the zest of a young lady at a bazaar, commanding the largest coins out of the purses of his young fellow-nobles; and when at last the whole market had been ransacked, yet the few remaining brooms still fell short of the number of despairing courtiers bent on gaining an audience, he put them up to auction, and forced the impatient gentlemen to bid one against other. 'Excellent broom this! heather closely cut. Twelve guildern did your Excellency say? Fourteen, your High Mightiness? Here's a stout broom-stick in case any lady housewife should need a little discipline. "Sixteen," said the Signior Capitano-Generale?'

'Come, come, Egmont,' was the impatient answer. 'We have no time for foolery, I must see the Emperor. Here's a couple of ducats and have done with it!'

'Two ducats! will no one go beyond that? Excellent heather broom,' and as the Signior Capitano muttered ugly words, 'What said his Excellency, three ducats? Knocked down to his Excellency il Signior Capitano-Generale Orsini, for three ducats!'

So went on the self-elected auctioneer, young Count Egmont, till the last broom, an old worn-out stump which he had actually pounced upon in a gutter, was disposed of for no less than seven Spanish dollars to a magnificently attired Cardinal in all his purple!

Peter's gains proved to be sufficient, in those days when the value of money was high, to make the little hut a substantial Flemish farmhouse, purchase cows, horses and tools, and, in short, to provide such a home as Doucette could be taken to as a happy bride, when she left the Countess d'Espinay in the spring.

THE TRAVELS OF TWO KITS.

Pussy cat, pussy cat, where have you been?
I've been to London to see the good queen.
Pussy cat, pussy cat, what saw you there?
I saw a little mouse under the chair.

THE TRAVELS OF TWO KITS.

My daughter tells me that though my grandchildren have so many charming little gilt books written on purpose for them, there is nothing they care for so much as for the story of their grandmamma's journey to London, in the days of good Queen Anne, and that they would like to have it written out for them, that she may read it to them as often as they wish. Therefore, I will do my best to set the whole down in order for them; but they must excuse it if I make mistakes, for I had no such education as they are blessed with. In truth, I knew nothing but how to read and sew until I was quite a great girl. Nobody taught me after my mother died, except that I went for a little while to a school that old Dame Redford kept in the village; but I could read as well as any of her scholars, and Nurse thought that I learnt country words, and rude manners there, such as were not becoming to the daughter of Sir Christopher Theobald, and so she took me away.

I was nearly seven years old when my mamma

died, and my little brother was only a week old. My poor father could not bear to look at either of us. I remember running up to him as he sat in his chair at the breakfast table with his hands over his face, and trying to pull them down and make him kiss me; but he only groaned and cried out, 'Take her away. I cannot endure the sight,' and then he stamped with his foot, so that I thought he was angry, and ran away crying.

Then Nurse Malkin did her best to comfort me, and told me I was not naughty, but that my poor papa was too unhappy to know what he did, and she let me hold the baby, which always made me content. I loved Nurse Malkin. She had been a maid at the Hall when I was a very little child, and had often played with me, before she married Farmer Malkin, and now she had come to be foster-mother to our poor little baby, and was to take him to Clover Farm to bring up with her own child. Seeing that my father could not bear the very sight of me, our cousin Reynold Theobald proposed that I should go with her likewise, which I was very glad to do, for Nurse Malkin was always kind, and no one at the Hall seemed to want me, or know what to do with me, and it was all so sad now my dear mamma was gone.

There came a clergyman in a gown and bands, with a wig on, and he christened my little brother by the name of Christopher. And he laid his hand on my head, and blessed me, and pitied me, and said I did not know what I had lost. Then Nurse Malkin tied on my little black hood and mantle, and walked up with the baby in her arms, and said, 'Bless your children, Sir Christopher.'

He looked up, and he tried to speak, with a hand on each of our heads, but he could only sob and weep, so that I burst out crying again, and Cousin Reynold hurried us away into a coach that was waiting at the hall door, and away we went, while the Church bell was tolling, and Nurse crying bitterly, for my dear mamma was to be buried that day.

Clover Farm was in the midst of grass fields, and there were belonging to it thirty fine cows, whose milk was saved for making cheese. I liked running about there, feeding the fowls and ducks, and finding the eggs, or watching the milking of the cows; and whenever she had time, Nurse Malkin made me read a bit in the Bible or Prayerbook, and sew, or knit, or spin; though she could not read herself. She took care of my manners too. I always sat at the head of the table, and she made me eat nicely with my knife and fork, not as the milkmaids and plough-boys did at the other end; and my brother and I were always called Little Master and Little Missy, till most people forgot that our true names were Christopher and Katharine.

For we did not see our father again for many years. He went away two or three days after the funeral, without having been able to make up his mind to look at us poor motherless children, to go and visit my mother's father and mother. They had followed King James II. when he fled from England, and were living at St. Germain's in France, and my father only meant to make them a visit and tell them about the death of their daughter; but when he was once gone, he could not come back again. I did not understand it then; I only knew that I grew tired of the life at the Farm, as the days grew short, and the farm-yard was all one swamp, so that Nurse would not let me run out. I used to fret and ask when we should go home, and she always answered, 'when my papa came back.' And if I asked 'When would that be?' she said something I never could make out about God's will, and evil men.

So the time went on, and the winter was over, but still my papa never came. Farmer Malkin was a hard gruff man, who never took much notice of us, except to scold me for doing mischief; and indeed I could hardly do anything that he did not call mischief. If I climbed a hay-cock, I spoilt the hay; if I played with the calves, I scared them; and I could not even hug the kitten but he said I should spoil it for a good mouser. Indeed, after poor little Will, our Kit's foster-brother, died in teething, I think he quite hated us both, and that was why Nurse sent me to school that I might be out of his way.

Still we stayed on at the Farm, for when he went up to the Hall to pay his rent, Cousin Reynold, who managed everything, threw him back something for our board and lodging. Cousin Reynold was a lawyer in London, but he came down twice a year to take the rents and see about the estate, and he used to write to my father, and send him money abroad. I heard the old people talk of Reynold's having lived at the Hall when my grandfather was away in Oliver Cromwell's time, and how hard a man he had been, so that all had feared him and rejoiced to have their old landlord back again.

So five years went away, and we were still living on at Clover Farm. Nurse had had another baby of her own by that time, and though she was never unkind, I do not think she cared for 'Little Master' nearly so much after the new comer was born; and the Farmer was quite cross and rough to my brother when he fretted and cried. Poor little dear, he often did, for he was a sickly little fellow, and often nothing would please him or make him happy, whatever I could do. Sometimes he could not eat the food at dinner, and then the Farmer would mutter about a beggarly brat having no right to be nice; sometimes he woke up screaming at night, and if I did not rush up and stop him in time,

Master Malkin would threaten him with the rod ; and if ever he played with even the hay and the straw, he would be found fault with and sometimes beaten. Nobody really cared for the poor little dear but myself, and he was all I had, so I loved him with all my heart and soul. I carried him about, gave him rides on the donkey, which had come from the Hall for our use, and was our own. I kept him out of the Farmer's way, and when we could curl up together in a corner, and he would stroke my face, and call me his Kitty, we were happy.

But when he was five years old, he began to get worse rather than better. It was a wet spring, and the floods were out all over the fields ever so long, and there were thick white fogs lying about the valleys. Kit went on catching cold, and wherever he cut or bruised himself there came a bad sore place which seemed as if it would never get well. He was always a thin pale child, with great brown eyes that seemed too big for his face, and now he grew thinner and whiter than ever, and seemed shrunk away just to nothing, so that I could lift and carry him about as easily as I could sturdy little Nancy, who was three years younger.

There was not much thought of doctors in our parts, except for great folks, but there was a wise woman at Southernhay, who had great skill in herbs ; and at last one day, Dame Malkin took Kit to see her. The master had gone to Bath, for Mr. Theobald had ordered him to give him the meeting there. He was not expected at home for three days, or I do not believe poor Nurse would have ventured so far, lest he should say she was wasting time and money, but I begged her so hard to try to get someone to cure my poor little brother of that sore in his neck, that she said she would try it.

We put Kit and Nancy into the two panniers on the donkey, and Nurse and I trudged a long way by its side, taking our food with us, till at last we came to a little low hovel, almost sunk in the side of a hill, where there was a goat browsing on the grass that grew on the roof, and an old woman in a little pointed hat, sitting at the door, spinning with a distaff, for wheels had not come in then.

Kit screamed, and I was a little afraid, but she was not a witch, though she looked like one. The parson knew her well, and she was a real godly woman who always came to Church. She had learnt her skill from having lived with a great lady, who was a herbalist, and had got her learning from Sir Walter Raleigh when he was in the Tower. She spoke very kindly and tenderly so that Kit forgot his fear, and let her lift him down, and give him some nice sweetened elder wine and water; and he sat quite happily in her lap, and let her look at the place in his neck. Then she put some ointment to it, which he said was 'good, good,' and presently he fell asleep in her lap.

Nurse and I were much pleased, and begged to know what she would take for a pot of the ointment. She said we might either give her one of our cheeses, or else half a crown, but that she would be true and faithful with us. 'Poor lamb,' she said, 'it ain't ointments as can do him good for long. It will only be healing it in one place for it to break out in another. There's nothing that cures this disease but the King's or Queen's touch, and couldn't ye get the poor child to London to be touched by Queen Anne, bless her?'

Nurse began to cry and say there was no hope then, for though we were quality children, our father was over the water, and his lands were managed by one that did not wish us well, and it was as good as giving up the child for lost.

But I opened my eyes wide, for there was a little chap-book at home, that I had bought of a pedlar with a new penny, which told how good King Edward the Confessor had given his hand to help a poor leprous beggar, and how in the night he had seen a vision that told him that he and his heirs should for ever have the power of healing diseases, with but a touch of the right hand. So I said, 'My little brother shall go to London to see the Queen, if you will only tell me the way.'

Then they both laughed and called me 'poor little Missy,' which vexed me much, for I was eleven years and seven months old, and almost as tall as Nurse.

Their laughing could not put it out of my mind. I knew which was the road to London, for once we had gone in the coach to meet my papa, when he was coming back from thence, and I was sure that all we had to do was to go on, and on, and ask the way. I told Nurse so as we came home, but she only said, 'Lawk a day, what will the child say next?'

I wished I could ask someone what to do, but the farming men knew less than Nurse; and as to the parson, we only saw him when he came once in three Sundays to the Church, where we went, if it was not too wet to walk the half mile to it. He was not like the clergyman who used to talk to my mamma, and say grace for us; he had a red face, and a wig like a cauliflower, and I never looked at him if I could help it. The only time I ever heard him speak except in Church was after he had christened little Nancy. Then he asked who we were, and when Nurse told him, 'Poor Sir Christopher's children,' he growled like a dog, and said, 'Jacobite spawn.' So I was not likely to get help from him, and all our own old servants had been turned out of the Hall, and strangers of Cousin Reynold's had been put in, who spoke so uncivilly that we never went up to the Hall.

The day after our visit to the wise woman, the farmer came home, and with him came, likewise riding, Cousin Reynold. His horse was led away by his servant, and he came striding into the kitchen and sat down.

'Oh! so these are the children, are they? Come here, mistress Kitty. Do you remember me?'

I made my curtsey and bridled, as my dear mamma had taught me, whenever a gentleman or lady spoke to me, and said, 'Yes, sir; I hope my papa is well.'

'Oh yes,' he said, 'and finding it convenient to stay in foreign parts. Do you write to him, child?'

'No, sir,' I said, and how my face burnt. 'I cannot write, but I think my papa would wish me to learn.'

'It shall be seen to,' he said. 'You grow a great lass, and it is time you were set to learn to do something for yourself. And this is the boy. Come here, sirrah.'

Of course Kit would not come, but clung crying behind my skirts, and kicked when Nurse tried to pull him away. The Farmer declared he was the most rude and troublesome child he had ever seen, always fractious and sickly.

Then I broke out. 'Cousin Reynold,' I said, 'our papa trusted us to Farmer Malkin, and this is the way he speaks of my poor little brother! Little Master is not naughty or fractious, but he is weak and sickly, and the good woman says nothing will cure him but the Queen's touch. Our papa would wish us to be taken to London that the Queen may touch him.'

I believe that was what I said. I know that the man broke out into a horrid derisive laugh. 'Ho, ho! you crow loud for a barn-door fowl, Mistress Katharine! What would Sir Christopher say to his son being touched by a usurper? 'Tis the King at St. Germain he would have his son taken to.'

I knew, by his voice, he was but mocking me; I would have no more of it. I made him my lowest curtsey, such as I used to make long ago, when my mamma taught me to dance the minuet, and I walked off, taking Kit with me, followed by still louder laughter.

We ran away as hard as Kit's little legs would go, as soon as we were out of sight. I did not choose to be called back to the fellow again who had thus insulted us, so I took Kit to my favourite hiding-place, the hay-loft over the stable, where no one ever thought of looking for us. It was hard work to drag him up the ladder, but when we were there, I made him a nest in the hay, and comforted him till he fell asleep in my lap.

By and by, I heard voices below. Cousin Reynold had come with the Farmer to look at the colt, but that was not all they were talking about. I heard Farmer Malkin say, 'Then, however, you'll let me have the lease of the farm at the lower terms. 'Tis but fair, I'm sure, after the trouble me and my dame have had with that there lad and lass.'

'Well, that will be over soon. I hear their father is on the point of volunteering in the French army, and that will cut him off for ever from returning, even if he be not knocked on the head by Prince Eugene or some of them! Then as to the boy, anyone can see he is not long for this world, and as soon as he has puled himself out of it, we will have the girl apprenticed to a mantua maker, or some other honest trade.'

What a hearing was this for me! Nothing but the fear of wakening my poor little brother, and making him betray us by crying, prevented me from hugging him desperately. I thought we were, indeed, the children in the wood, our cousin the cruel uncle, and Farmer Malkin and his wife the two murderers. Even Nurse seemed to me no better than the ruffian milder in mood, and I made up my mind, while still sitting in that loft, that nothing should hinder me from myself taking my little brother to London to receive the royal touch. I was sure that the people about us wished him to die rather than live, and there was no safety for him but in getting him away. If I thought at all about what was to come after, I varied between notions of making our way to my father, and of maintaining Kit and myself by selling watercresses in the streets.

It was too late to set off that day, even when Cousin Reynold was safe gone. I saw his horse being saddled, through the chinks in the floor, and I heard Nurse's voice calling 'Missy and Master' all over the farm-yard, that we might come and wish our cousin good-bye, but Kit did not waken, and I took good care not to stir till he was gone, and Farmer Malkin with him for part of the way.

When we came down Nurse Malkin began scolding me for hiding away, but I drew up my head and told her I was not going to stand there to be insulted.

Then she began to cry with her apron over her head, and to wish she had never seen the day, and to declare that she had only wished for my good, for them that had the power wanted to be spoken fair. And then Kit declared that the nasty man should be shot with his gun, which only made her sob the more, and take him in her arms and call him her dear lamb. Thinking her not after all even the milder ruffian, I ventured to say, 'What did Cousin Reynold mean by saying my papa would have us go to the King at St. Germains?'

'Meant! meant! Why, nowt but his own wicked devices,' broke out Nurse. 'As though I hadn't heard poor Sir Christopher drink health to King William and Queen Mary, and he would no doubt to this here Queen Anne, if it weren't for the cruel lies of them as keeps him from his own place that is his right! Lawk a day, is that the master? Hush you up, Missy, this moment, or what will he do to us?'

Nothing more was wanting to settle my mind. It was May, and the days were long and fine. There was a great deal of cheese-making going on, and we were much left to ourselves except that we were burdened with the care of Nancy, who always cried to run after us. Lately her father had taken to saying that, if I was of no other use, I might at least mind the child, and this made me very angry, for I certainly had not been sent to Clover Farm to act as his nursemaid. I was proud and angry, my dears, I do not hide it, for I knew little that was good. I said my prayers at night as my mamma had taught me, and made my brother do so too, when he would, and on a Sunday, Nurse tried to make me say the Catechism, but she scarce knew it herself, and the long words used to run into nonsense.

I knew that I must choose my opportunity either before Nancy was up in the morning, or while she was asleep in the forenoon. It was quite impossible, I found, to get off in the morning, for all the men and maids were astir by four o'clock, milking and turning out the cows; but I was able in the meantime to roll up a change of linen for each of us, and to climb up to the corner where, in the bottom of an old broken India china jar, nurse had stowed away my beautiful pocket piece, a five-guinea piece of King Charles II. It was rolled up in a curious-looking paper with writing on it, and a great *One* in the corner. I remembered my mamma saying, 'Give it to Kitty, it shall be kept for a curiosity.' So I took it with me, put it in a little bag, and hung it round my neck, and likewise a crown-piece inside the bosom of my frock, and two shillings that Nurse had kept, when the pedlar changed my one gold guinea for her to buy me a frock. I was glad of the silver now, for the pedlar had made a work about changing the guinea, and I knew it might be hard to use my pocket piece; besides that, I did not want to part with it, so I put them into a little box in my pocket.

We broke our fast on milk porridge at six o'clock, and then Nurse and all her maids went off to the cheese room. I thought Nancy never would have gone to sleep that day, but at last she did, for it was very hot. Kit was asleep too, but that mattered less, and I was able to pack a little basket with Kit's ointment, and some bread and cheese, and a bit of bacon. I did not think it was stealing, as our board was paid for. I caught the donkey in the yard, and put on his halter, for we cared for nothing else, being used to ride him bare-backed.

Then, all being ready, and our hats and cloaks laid under the hedge, I came back and fetched Kit, telling him I would take him to London to see the good Queen and be made well. But as we came to the door, what should the child do but call out for his mousie? He could not leave his mousie behind. One of the farm boys had brought him a dormouse, rolled up in a ball, and he loved and cared for it better than anything else. I knew he would break out in loud crying if mousie were left, so I could only jump up and take down the little earthen jar where we kept it, in a bed of moss. He was quiet when he knew mousie was going with him, and I led him safely to the nook under the hedge, where the donkey stood. He had on his little leather breeches, the grey stockings I had knitted for him, and his best blue coat, not at all what a young gentleman as he was should have worn, but that turned out well for us in the end. His long light hair hung on his neck, I never could make it curl, and I put on his hat, and gave it a cock. I laid his cloak and mine on the donkey's neck, for it was too hot to use them then. And I put on my own Sunday hat of felt, high-crowned and broad-brimmed. I had my grey every-day frock, I durst not take out my Sunday one, and it was not much better, only newer and less faded.

I knelt down, and made Kit kneel down and say, 'Bless our journey, O God, and keep us in the way. Amen;' and then I lifted him up on the donkey, took the halter, and we set out.

I knew we must cross the park and get out on the Warminster road, and that was done without difficulty. I led the donkey, and when Kit grew fretful and tired, we crept into the wood out of sight, and ate our food. He wanted drink, and I knew where one of the lodges was. The keeper's mother, a kind old woman, gave us some milk, and said, ' Dear, dear, you didn't ought to be so far from home, little Miss and little Master. Dame Malkin will be in a way about you. Get you home as soon as you can. I wish Tom was in to go with you. That I do!'

That I did not, and I took Kit, and as quick as I could for fear that either she should say we were not going home, or that Tom should come back.

We had kept to byways instead of crossing the

park, where we could be seen by the windows, and it was four o'clock at least, when at last we were out of it, and I found my feet on the hard ruts on the high road. It was very hot, and I was tired already; but I thought if I gave up so soon, how should I ever reach London? When Kit began to fret, I scrambled up behind him on the donkey, and tried to comfort him, though my heart began to sink as I thought, how should we contrive to rest for the night?

Presently we saw, on the open side of the road, a number of gipsies resting and eating their supper, We were both dreadfully afraid of gipsies, and Kit threw his arms round me, and began to scream so loud that all our chance of slipping by them unseen was over. Out came numerous dogs and children and women, all gathering round us, while Kit clung to me and shrieked.

'Whisht, whisht, my pretty darling, I won't hurt thee,' said one of the women, with fierce black eyes, and long gold earrings under her bright yellow kerchief. 'My pretty maid, ye'll cross my hand with silver, and hear yer fortune?'

And when I begged her to let us go on, not able to hide the trembling of my voice, she laid hold of the halter of the donkey, stood full in our way, and demanded where we were going. 'To London. Do let me go,' I said.

'O ho! Ye've run away, my lass,' she said, her eyes looking me through, so that I thought she knew all by her magic power, and that it was of no use to conceal anything.

'Yes,' I said, 'I am taking my little brother to see the Queen, and be cured by her touch! O pray, good woman, let us go on.'

'Yes, yes,' she said in a more wheedling tone. 'We'll put you on your way, my dear. Come you on with us.'

'We had rather go alone,' I said. She assured me that I should miss the way, fall in with thieves, and I know not what besides, and at the same time she had firm hold of the donkey's halter, so that we were her prisoners.

Most likely she thought we were runaway farmer's children, and her purpose was to carry us out of reach of rescue or pursuit, in case our home was near, for she kept on in her coaxing way, as the whole party moved on, carts, rough ponies, donkeys, rough wild men, barefooted children, dogs and all. When I made an effort to get free, she raised a great stick and threatened me. Then I knew that we were stolen by gipsies, and a terror and almost a cold sickness came over me as I recollected stories that I had heard, and as I thought of my dear little tender brother, the one thing I cared for, being bred up to be a thief and a vagabond, all stained with walnut juice. I implored her to let us go, and Kit cried bitterly, but she told us to hold our noise; and on, and on, and on, we went, till it began to grow dark; and, meantime, Kit had grown so weary that he could only moan and could not keep upright on the donkey, and my legs were so tired and my feet so sore, that I could only limp and shuffle along. Then the gipsies tumbled us into a cart among some straw, and I fancy some little children of their own. We slept, feeling all through our sleep the bumping and jolting. By and by, there was a stop in the dark; I was hauled out, and half asleep, took Kit in my arms, as he was handed after me, and tried to hush his crying. Happily he did not wake up enough to take it all in; and I could hardly stand, I was so stiff with sleep. We both slept again almost instantly, and never woke again till it was broad daylight, and then we found ourselves quite alone under the dewy hedge on the side of the hill. Gipsies, children, horses, dogs and all were gone, and what was worse, our poor donkey.

I imagine that the design of the gipsies all along had been to steal the poor ass, and that this was the reason they had taken us so far from where they found us, and left us sleeping, that we might not give the alarm till they had gone out of reach. We did not look worth kidnapping. I was too old, and my brother too sickly, and there was nothing about us to show that we were not little rustics of the better class.

They had carried off our cloaks, and had rifled my pocket of the silver crown and the shilling, but they had never suspected that I had a gold piece in my bosom, and had not meddled with the clothes we wore. Indeed they were not wholly cruel, for they had left us my basket with Kit's pot of ointment, and mousie in his jar, and had even put in the basket a great piece of oaten cake.

Kit began to cry when he found we were in a strange place all alone, but I was so glad the gipsies were gone that I felt quite happy and hopeful; I showed Kit his mouse, which comforted him a little, and made him kneel and say his prayers. Then I gave him some of the oat cake. It was rough and dry, but we were terribly hungry; and as we ate it, we held one another by the hand, and crept along, hoping to recover our ass. Then, indeed, I found myself so footsore that my heart failed me as to how I should ever get along myself, to say nothing of Kit, if poor Jack were indeed gone. Alas! we could find him no where. I knew not where we were. Everything was quite still, except that a lark was singing merrily away high up in the sky, so merrily that I felt as if he were laughing at me. I longed to sit down and cry, but what would become of Kit if I did so?

Just at that moment, I caught a sound of someone singing, and there was something friendly in the sound. It was not a milk-maid's morning song, but it gave me the feeling as if I were going to Church with my papa and mamma as in the olden times. I limped on towards the sound, which grew clearer, and I presently distinguished that it was a Psalm Tune and a man's voice, an old's man's voice, though very sweet, and almost as blithe as that of the lark, and these words were the first I heard distinctly:—

> Wake and lift up thyself my heart,
> And with the Angels bear thy part,
> Who all night long unwearied sing
> High praise to the Eternal King.
>
> Awake, awake, ye heavenly choir;
> May your devotion me inspire,
> That I like you my age may spend,
> Like you may on my God attend.

Just then we came beyond the hedge, and this is what we saw through an opening. There were trees falling back on either side of a steep slope, almost a cliff of green grassy turf, beneath which lay the level ground of a park, studded with magnificent trees, reaching to a fine house, beyond which lay a beautiful undulating country of wood and park and field, rising to very high ground, and all lighted up by the rays of the morning sun, which made everything sparkle, while the trees were in the youngest, freshest green. You know the place, my dears, it is what is called Heaven's Gate. And in front, on the top of the cliff, stood a slight old man, with his back to us, his grey hair coming out beneath his black velvet cap, and in a clergyman's gown. That gave me courage, I was sure that I had found a helper, and I went forward with Kit, and knelt down on the grass, as we had been taught to do, to ask his blessing; but he was so wrapt in his devotion that he did not see us. The sun shone on his face; and when I hear the Lesson read of the glory of Moses's countenance when he had been communing with the Lord on Mount Sinai, I always think of the face of the holy Bishop Ken as we saw him on that morning. For he it was, though I knew nothing about him then. His look, and his hymn, seemed to take me away from myself and my troubles, and I would have knelt on, happy in hearing and watching him; but little Kit, growing impatient, plucked his gown, and made him look down, when I put my hands over my face as in the good old days and said, 'Your blessing, sir.'

He put one of his long slender hands on each of our heads and blessed us. And then he said kindly, seeing perhaps Kit's tear-stained face, 'And whence have you come, my little ones, to ask an old man's blessing?'

'Oh! sir, help us,' I said. 'I am taking my little brother to London to be touched by the Queen, and the gipsies have stolen our donkey, and we have lost our way, and we don't know what to do!' And there, though I tried to stop myself, I could not help bursting into tears.

The good Bishop must have been very much surprised, but he said, 'Come, come, my little dear, we will have no crying. Come with me to the house yonder,' and he took a hand of each of us. 'You shall break your fast, and then you shall tell me where you come from, and I will let your friends know.'

'O no, sir,' I cried. 'We have no friends except our father over the sea! And Nurse Malkin would stop us!'

Then he asked our names; and when we told them, he stood still with amazement, and said, 'The children of Sir Christopher Theobald of Catlinch Hall?' And when we replied, he said, 'I know your honoured father, my children, and your good mother. I have been at Catlinch Hall, and I have seen you before, Mistress Katharine, though you do not know it.'

Then as a man-servant came out to meet him and

say 'his lordship's breakfast was served,' he bade him carry Master Theobald. I think he would have done so himself long before he knew us, seeing how the poor little fellow lagged, but that he was an old man and had scarcely strength. Meanwhile, he held my hand, and I had told him all my story, by the time we came to the house of Longleat, where we found another clergyman at the door, the Reverend Mr. Harbin, who was chaplain.

Breakfast was ready in his room. It was of beef and ale, but the Bishop sent for some milk for us, and bade the servant ask the housekeeper to be good enough to come to speak with him. She came in curtseying low.

'Mistress Deborah,' he said, 'these are Miss and Master Theobald of Catlinch. They have been robbed by the gipsies, and have slept the night upon the ground, and I should hold myself much obliged if you would let them rest, and have attendance and comfort in one of the bedrooms, until dinner-time, when I request the favour of their company.'

'Only please sir, you will not send us back?' I entreated, ready to cry.

'Indeed, my little lady, you need not fear me. We will talk of what you will do next, after dinner. Go now, and rest with Mrs. Deborah.'

The housekeeper led us to a beautiful large room,

as fine as our best at home, and the maids brought warm water, and we were undressed and made very comfortable. She pitied Kit very much, and asked us many questions, thinking we had been stolen from home; but she looked grave when she found we had run away, and I feared again that we should be sent back. However, I was stiff and tired, and not at all unwilling to lie down by Kit on the big state bed, and try to make out the stories in the tapestry in a dreamy kind of way, till nearly one o'clock, when Mrs. Deborah came back, and we were made ready for dinner. I know now that though the good Bishop had taken us at our word directly, there were some who doubted my story, or whether two such shabby beggarly-looking children could belong to Sir Christopher Theobald. Thus it was very well for us that Nurse had bred me up to nice ways, for Mrs. Deborah afterwards said she had no misgivings after I took out my ivory comb, and put my own hair, and Kit's, in order for dinner, making his little lovelock hang over his shoulder, shining like silk; and he was as good as gold, and made his bow as I told him, when we came down, waving his hat as prettily as could be.

Then, when the Bishop said that little master should be chaplain, I had but to give him a hint, and he said his grace. I cut his meat and spread his napkin, and he behaved himself like a little gentleman as he was, all through the dinner. More than once I saw nods pass between the Bishop and Mr. Harbin, which meant, I believe, that we were no impostors, but of gentle blood and breeding. I knew my manners better than to ask for anything, or to speak at table, except when I was addressed; and though Kit broke out with a little cry of joy when he saw a great bowl of custard and strawberries, he was so little that it did not matter.

After dinner, the Bishop led us out into the flower-garden behind the house; and he told me that he saw I was a good little maid, and careful of my brother, and that he was sure that I had been taught my duty. Then he said he should like to know if I could say the Catechism. I could only go very red and say I did not know it well; for Nurse could not say it herself, and I had not learnt it all when my mamma died. However, I made a shift to repeat the Creed, and though I stumbled through the Commandments, and did not know their numbers, still he said I was doing well, if I were trying to act them out; and that he would teach me a fresh prayer to say, fitter than the baby one I was used to. He was so gentle that he never frightened me at all, but I felt almost as if I had my papa again; and Kit sat on his knee all the time playing with his watch and seals.

After that he called Mr. Harbin, and they questioned me over again, much more closely, about Reynold Theobald and Farmer Malkin, and my plans for running away. I would have shown them Kit's neck, but they said Mrs. Deborah had told them how bad it was, and that I was a good child for wishing to take him to the Queen, only that I must remember it was not she, but God, who wrought cures.

The Bishop said he would not send us back, nor help Mr. Theobald to lay hands on us. He would only let Nurse know that we were safe; and he would help us on our way. The next day the stage-waggon would pass on the way to London, and he knew the carrier to be a good and careful man, to whom he would commit us, with a charge to deliver us to one Mrs. Boardman, a friend of his in Fenchurch Street, to whom he would give us a letter, praying her to take care of us, lodge us, and bring us to the Chapel Royal of St. James's when the Queen should be touching for the Evil, as she did several times in the summer months.

'And, my lord,' I said, (Mrs. Deborah had told me how to call him) 'I could pay my way, if I could get my pocket-piece changed, but the gipsies took my new crown-piece.'

Then I pulled out the string, and the Bishop said he would change the gold piece, and keep it for me, for maybe I should like to redeem it in time to come. And so I have done, and I have left it in my will to my brother's eldest son.

He sent us away with a young servant-maid to play in the garden, and we did not see him again that night, but in the morning, we broke our fast with him, and went to prayers in the Chapel, and these were scarce over before a groom, who had been set to watch, brought word that Will Carrier was at the foot of the hill.

Mrs. Deborah had done wonders for us. She had found two outgrown cloaks of Lord Weymouth's children, she had sought out a large soft cushion on which Kit might lie, she had packed my basket with slices of bread and meat, with gooseberry pasties and strawberries, and she had given Kit a cage for his mouse, in which he could see the little creature, and keep him far more safely than in our jar.

She kissed us, and gave all these things to one of the servants to carry; and even then she put on her hood and pattens, for she must come out to settle us in the waggon herself. However, the waggon had turned out of the way and was coming up to the hall, so soon as Will Carrier understood that my Lord Bishop wanted him.

It was a big broad-wheeled waggon, painted blue, with red wheels, and covered with an arched tilt, under which, as in the mouth of a deep cavern, sat Will Carrier, with his honest ruddy face and curly hair, ruling over the four strong broad-chested horses that drew us, two abreast, two of them black, and two dapple grey.

He took off his slouched hat as he approached, and, leaping down from his perch, made a low obeisance as his lad stood at the horses' heads, while he asked what commands his lordship had.

The Bishop and Mr. Harbin then committed us to his care, and he engaged to make us over to Mrs. Boardman, as well as to see that we were well fed, lodged, and attended to upon the way. Indeed he said he had a good dame in his waggon, going up from Glastonbury to live with her son in London, and that no doubt she would have an eye to us. I think the Bishop, when he thought I was not looking, gave both the carrier and the woman some money to attend to us, and then he kissed my little brother, and blessed us both, and gave me a thick letter to deliver to Mrs Boardman, and so away we went.

It was comfortable in the waggon, all the larger boxes and bundles were piled up in the end, and there were seats across, besides a square space behind where the driver sat. When Kit was tired, I laid him down on his cushion on the bottom of the waggon, and he slept. Sometimes people got in to go a stage or two, but no one went the whole way except Mrs. Lee, and she was very kind to us, and used to tell us stories as we went slowly along between the hedges. Sometimes we got down to have a run, when we were going between flowery banks, where we could gather posies, and sometimes the carrier would lift Kit up, and give him a ride on the broad back of one of his horses. We used to halt three times a day, for breakfast, dinner, and supper, besides the putting up for the night; generally at way-side inns, standing on village greens, where Kit and I were taken into the parlour, with a sanded floor, and peacock's feathers over the mantel shelf, and they gave us nice bowls of milk, and fresh fruit. Sometimes we found in the evening parties of gentlemen playing at bowls outside; and when we had had our supper, and Kit had been put to sleep in the white curtained bed with sheets smelling of lavender, I used to stay up longer, standing in the deep bay window to watch the game, which my father used to play on our own bowling green at home.

At one inn, the last but one I think, where we slept before reaching London, we were close to the broad beautiful river Thames, and there I saw two gentlemen fishing by the river's bank. In the morning at breakfast there was a beautiful dish of broiled fish with Mr. Izaak Walton's service to Mistress and

Master Theobald, and he hoped that they had left the good Bishop Ken in good health. Mrs. Lee told us that he had been so polite as to leave the parlour for us, and that it would be due courtesy to invite him and his friend to breakfast with us. So I did, and they came in, making such reverences and thanks that I scarcely knew which way to look, and they were very kind and good, giving us a beautiful box of comfits to eat upon the road.

At last we come in through the streets of London. Kit looked out to see them paved with gold and silver, but they seemed to me even fouler and dirtier than the streets of Warminster on a wet day. There were throngs of people, and carts and great folk's coaches, painted and gilt, with four and six horses, so choking up the ways that Will Carrier had much ado to get along to the great inn-yard where he put up in London. Mrs. Lee kissed us and bade us good-bye, and then the carrier brought us through the streets to Mrs. Boardman's house, taking Kit in his arms, while I was fain to cling to his carter's frock where the crowd was thickest. Even so I had like to have been knocked into the gutter by a great beam they were carrying to build one of the new Churches in the City.

Mrs. Boardman was the widow of an Alderman, and lived in a house of her own with a paved court in front and a lilac and laburnum tree in the midst, the first we had ever seen, and Kit cried out 'There, there, it is true! there's a tree dropping gold;' and he wanted to be set down to pick up the blossoms.

Will Carrier knocked at the door, and when a man came out, he said he had commands from the Lord Bishop at Longleat and that he must speak with the mistress herself. We waited in a wainscoted chamber, panelled with some sweet foreign woods, and polished like the inside of a workbox, with a little round table, and a big china beaupot in the middle.

Mrs. Boardman came down in her shining black taffeta gown, with a long waist, and the skirt tucked through the pocket holes, showing her quilted grey petticoat; she had a white apron, long white pinners and a white cap, and her face was as gentle as the Bishop's and looked like a mother's. She was lame and walked with a ivory-headed, crutch-handled cane, that went tap, tap, all down the stairs, before she came to us, then Will pulled his forelock, and said, 'My zarvice to you, Madam Boardman, and my Lord Bishop sends this here little Miss and Master to you. I was to zee them into your own hands, and Miss will tell you the rest. Mayhap ye'd give me a line to zartify to his Reverence as how they be delivered in good condition.'

'Well and good, Master Carrier,' said Mrs. Boardman. 'If you will wait a few minutes, Peter shall bring you a draught of ale, and I will talk with this young gentlewoman, and write the acknowledgment you wish. Anyone recommended by my Lord Bishop must be welcome.'

Then I went forward to ask the carrier for his account. He had it all scored on a tally, for the Bishop had bidden him pay for us at all the inns, and the sum came to three pounds five shillings and six pence, which I duly paid him, and I thanked him for having been so good to us. Kit clung to him, and kissed him, and said he would like to ride on broad-backed Dobbin again; while Will Carrier said he would never forget us, and he would like to have such travellers every time.

Then he went away, and Mrs. Boardman took us into her parlour, which was wainscoted likewise, but had a bay window looking into a garden, and a Turkey carpet under our feet, the like of which for softness we had never trod. She gave us each a little cricket to sit upon, and a piece of plum cake to eat, while she cut round the big seal of the Bishop's letter, and sat down to read it, putting on her spectacles. Presently she began sighing, 'Dear heart! Bless me!' and at last she broke out, 'Well, this is a strange thing! You don't mean to tell me that a mere slip of a girl like you, saving your presence, my young lady, set out to take this child all the way from Somerset to London!'

And when she had heard the story and understood the letter, she fell to kissing us both, and promising that she would do all that in her lay to bring us to the Queen, and that in the meantime we should be as welcome in her house as flowers in May. But already Kit was much better and stronger and rosier, though the place on his neck was not yet well.

There was another letter enclosed within Mrs. Boardman's, to the Court surgeon, asking him to give a ticket for Christopher Theobald, and to obtain for us admission to St. James's Palace. Mrs. Boardman sent this by her man Peter, and he brought back an answer that on Monday we should be at the Palace at eleven o'clock, and enclosing the paper with the name written on it. In the mean time, we were very happy with Mrs. Boardman. She was too lame to take us out, but we played in her garden, and on Sunday she went to Church, being carried in a sedan chair, in which she took Kit, while I trudged behind with her woman, whose name was Charity.

She was very good to us, and much wished to make us look more as the son and daughter of a baronet should look when before her Majesty, but Sunday intervening, there was no time to get us new suits of clothes, even if we had had the price of them, and she could only brush and mend our clothes up as far as was possible in one Friday and Saturday. Kit's hat was very shabby, but that mattered the less that he would be bareheaded before Her Majesty, and no one had finer or silkier hair than my little brother. What grieved me more was that good Mrs. Boardman could not go with us. She said she knew that she should have to stand for hours, and that was more than her poor leg would bear, and mayhap we should be better among the Quality by ourselves, than with any-one she could think of.

So she made Peter fetch a hackney coach, wherein we went, with Charity to take care of us on the way, and she waited in the coach outside the gates, while Peter with Kit in his arms, forced his way on through the throng, showing the ticket to the guards as we went. They say that poor children sometimes were pressed to death in the crowd or ever they came to the palace door ; and I can well believe it, for I never was so much frightened, not even by the gipsies, and if we had not been helped by a strong man like Peter, who knew the ways of a London crowd, we should never have come to the face of the Queen after all.

But pushing and squeezing, first up one step then another, we came to a doorway, and there Peter set Kit down and delivered me the ticket, saying, 'There, Mistress, I can go no farther, but I will wait for you outside, and call the coach when you come out. There will be no such throng then.'

The sentry, who had a scarlet coat, and tall pointed cap, let us through, and we followed, without further crowding, amongst some twenty or more women, some carrying, some leading, little children, through a lane of servants, till we came forth into the great banqueting-hall, where all the afflicted, and those who brought them, were ranged at the end of the hall.

There was a great chair of state at the upper end of the hall, and after we had stood long in waiting, all the great folks began coming in, the gentlemen in their velvet and laced coats, with embroidered waistcoats, curled white full-bottomed wigs, and diamond buckles in their shoes; and the ladies in their rustling brocades, with rich lace ruffles hanging to their waists. They all spread out in a semicircle, round the chair of state, and then in came the Queen herself, a portly and stately lady, with her hair dressed high and her gown of white satin, with a purple velvet train. She was handed in by a gentleman in a blue velvet coat with diamond buttons and a blue ribbon across his white waistcoat, and by her other side stood a tall lady with a long neck, light hair falling over it, a bright colour, and a face short, but very fair to look on. This was lady Marlborough, the Mistress of the Robes, the wife of the great General who was fighting in Bavaria.

Close by, at a desk a little in front were three clergymen in their robes and bands. One had a number of white ribbons with pieces of gold hanging to them, lying across his arm.

Then the service began. I need not tell you all, you can read it for yourselves in my large Prayer-book. It was not long, and after the Lord's Prayer had been said, the persons to be healed moved up, and one by one the Queen laid a white soft hand upon them, stroked them several times, and her lips moved in silent prayer as she bound one of the white ribbons from which the gold pieces were suspended, about the arms of each whom she touched, the chaplains going on with the prayers all the time. One or two were grown up persons, others were quite young children, carried by their mothers, and as I was not quite sure whether Kit was to go alone, or whether I was to lead him, he came last. Indeed he turned bashful, and would never have gone up at all, had I not been there to draw him on. Little did I think that the naughty boy had, unknown to me, carried his dormouse to Court in his bosom. When I unbuttoned his collar that the Queen might stroke his neck, I never guessed what would happen; but while she was hanging the gold piece upon his arm, he slipped down, with a cry of 'My mouse, my mouse!' and went on his hands and knees under the Queen's chair.

Up started the Queen in no small haste. The gentleman in the blue ribbon said, '*Est-il possible?*' Some of the ladies screamed, 'A mouse, a mouse!' and darted away as far as they could go with one skid before they bethought themselves where they were. Others lower down murmured, 'A Jacobite plot,' and one or two gentlemen near laid their hands on their swords, while others farther off drew them. Yet they frightened me even less than Lady Marlborough, who stood frowning, and saying, 'Remove the ill-nurtured little wretch, and let him be well flogged,' Kit did not hear her. He had wriggled out again, backwards, and regained his feet, and there he stood with his mouse in his hand, quite satisfied to have recovered it.

'Who is in charge of this boy?' demanded Lady Marlborough. 'Let him be taken away and well chastised.'

'Oh! Madam!' I cried, falling down on my knees, and putting my arm round Kit, 'spare him, I pray you. He knows no better. He is my little brother, and so frail and weak! Please beat me instead of him.'

'He is but a babe,' said the Queen more kindly,

looking down at him pitifully. 'The blame rests with those who have him in charge. Who are they?'

'Only I, ma'am—your Grace—your Majesty—' I scrambled out in desperate haste. 'I never guessed he had his mouse—and I brought him all the way from Somersetshire in hopes your most religious and gracious Majesty would touch him and cure him.'

'*Est-il possible?*' said the gentleman with the blue ribbon again.

Another gentleman here came forward saying, 'May it please your Majesty, I think these are the children respecting whom I have a letter from the retired Bishop of Bath and Wells. What is your name, young mistress?'

'I am Katharine Theobald, sir, and this is my little brother Christopher.'

'Even so,' said the gentleman, whom I found afterwards was Lord Weymouth, 'the children of Sir Christopher Theobald.'

'Impossible,' said the Queen. 'Sir Christopher Theobald is a gentleman of good estate—I knew him and his lady well—she was Lady Katharine Carshalton. How should her children be reduced to such a state as this? For in truth the girl reminds me of my old playmate. Do you not see the likeness, my dear Mrs. Freeman?' she added in an under tone, looking up to Lady Marlborough, who did not make much reply.

Then Lord Weymouth asked the Queen's leave to explain, and she granted it, seating herself on her chair again. He told, what I had never understood the half of before, namely, that our father had in his first grief for his wife's death, gone abroad to see her parents, who were living at Paris. He himself had never shown any lack of obedience to King William, but his kinsman, Reynold Theobald, in the hope of gain, had sent him false information that he was suspected of disloyalty, that a warrant was out against him, and that he could not safely return. Meanwhile Reynold had authority to manage the estate, he sent a yearly sum to my father, and kept us at Clover Farm.

'And thence,' Lord Weymouth explained, 'this brave young lady,' as he was pleased to call me, 'had set forth all alone, like a very Penthesilea,' (so he said) 'to bring her little brother to enjoy the benefits of the royal touch!'

'*Est-il possible?*' said the blue ribbon again.

Then happened the wonder of my life, for the good Queen held out both those white soft hands of hers, and the tears were in her eyes as she said, 'You are a good girl, Mistress Katharine,' and she kissed us both on the forehead.

'And you will not have Kit whipped,' I said hastily.

'No, no, indeed,' she said, her hand on his soft

hair; 'I love not whippings. Go, children. My Lord Weymouth, will you take them in charge. Have you more to say, my child?' she added.

'If your Majesty will only let my papa come home!' I said.

'There is nothing against him,' she said. 'My Lord Weymouth will see to it that Sir Christopher is summoned home. We cannot spare our loyal subjects to be exiled on a misapprehension.'

That is the chief of my story. I need scarce tell how we were lodged in Lady Weymouth's house with the Misses and Master Thynne, and how Kit's neck was entirely cured long before my father came home. I strove hard to learn all that the Misses Thynne knew, that I might not be a mere rustic when my father came; and Kit had grown plump and rosy, and when he had his new scarlet coat, silk stockings, and lace cravat, he looked such a darling little gentleman that my father when he came home, could at first do nothing but stand and say, 'Kitty, Kitty, you have indeed been a mother to that child!' And was I not a happy maiden?

SELMA'S SECRET SIGHS.

'Speech is silver, silence is golden.'

SELMA'S SECRET SIGHS.

My dear Lucy,

You said you could not understand what had gone amiss, and in the short time that we spent together it was impossible to explain, so I will profit by my present leisure to tell you the history.

You knew how happy my governess life at Fairleigh was. When I first was in negotiation with Mrs. Nutley, I thought I ought to mention my engagement, explaining that there was no chance of my seeing Bryan Arrowsmith at Fairleigh, nor of our being able to marry for years to come. Mrs. Nutley was quite satisfied, and there was no occasion for anybody else to know of it; nor did anyone, until there came to the Vicarage, as governess, no other than my dear old friend and school-fellow, Bryan's cousin, Aurelia Stillwood, who knew all, and to whom I could talk of Bryan—a delight for which I sometimes quite hungered.

Nor indeed was I disappointed. In the few hours we could spend alone together, there could not be a kinder or pleasanter listener than Aurelia, whose eyes and smile and soft little words were just enough to carry one on. She was just like what she had been at school, where she used to be called the Little Grey Mouse. She has the neatest of little figures, and dresses in soft greys and fawns, that never fade or spot with her as they do with ordinary mortals, with dainty white accompaniments, always crisply fresh; and her clear brown eyes shone out of their dark fringes and seemed to speak instead of her lips. Her pupils—a delicate boy, who could not be sent to school, and a little wild tomboy of a girl—were more devoted to her than suited me; for whenever we spent an afternoon together, and thought the children would amuse one another, Wilfred would always grow tired, and come to lie on the ground or the sofa, wanting her to stroke his forehead, and there ended all intimate conversation. Though I own the intimacy was chiefly on my side—for she never said a word about her pupils, or their tempers, not even to consult me, though I am a year older, and had had two years' more experience. She never asked my advice, except once when Wilfred's sum would not come right, and another time when there was a misprint in the grammar. I used often to tell her of my joys and trials with my three girls; and when I heard of Mrs. Halstead telling the story of Agnes being caught preaching a sermon in a pulpit of towel-horses, with a sheet for a surplice, and a scarlet comforter for a stole, and all her dolls for audience, I did think it hard that Aurelia had never told me, and I scolded her a little for it; but she said she thought it not fair to tell such things. So stupid, thought I, when there was no fear of my repeating them. Aurelia might trust me!

We two must have made a favourable impression; for one day Mrs. Nutley asked me to recommend another pupil from St. Katharine's to Mrs. Robinson for her little girls, just out of the nursery. I thought at once of my old crony, Sally Shilling—the merry eager girl, so clever and bright, and such a favourite with all—and I spoke of her merits so enthusiastically, that Mrs. Robinson wrote to her that very evening. I eagerly told Aurelia, and, in spite of my experience, was discomfited by her sober 'Indeed!'

'Don't you think her equal to such little scraps of children?' I asked, getting hot and frightened.

'Yes, I think she is.'

'Don't you think her good and high principled? Don't you remember how well she behaved about that key to the exercises?'

'Yes, she is very upright.'

'Do you mean that you think her too rough and ready?'

'Certainly not;' looking rather funny.

'Then what do you mean? Provoking girl! you are enough to distract one. Say it at once, if you know anything against her?'

'But I don't.'

'Then why in the world should you not be glad to see her?'

'I am glad.'

'Then why speak in that way?'

'What did I say?'

I had to examine, and confess that she had only said 'Indeed,' and then she smiled! But I remember maintaining that she ought to be more cordial, and then fearing that she thought the Robinsons would not be kind to Sally. However, she cleared herself of any such suspicion, and I was obliged to forgive her for her 'Indeed,' and think it only 'her way.'

Sally wrote a rapturous letter about her joy at being near the two dearest of her friends, and the compensation of our society in this melancholy position. It made me wonder whether any misfortune had happened to the Shillings, for Sally's family had always seemed to me a joyous one. To be sure the father was dead, but that had happened before anyone could recollect; and Mrs. Shilling was a capital manager, who paid the rent of her house in the City by letting the first floor to a curate, and who kept her sons together. They were excellent fellows; one was in an office, another walking the hospitals, and the other two at King's College and King's College School, while the youngest girl had just gone to St. Katharine's. I had sometimes spent a holiday among them, and their hearty good-nature and merriment always charmed me. Mrs. Shilling allowed that she preferred boys to girls, and was always full of business; but she looked after her daughters well, and I was grieved to think of her being in trouble. I asked Aurelia, if she knew what was amiss, but she could not guess. I wondered, too, at the signature of the letter.

'Selina?' I said; 'I had always thought her name was Sarah!'

'So it is: Sarah Mary.'

'The letter is certainly hers! but Selina alone is not exactly a signature, with no surname!'

'It is not Selina, but Selma!'

'A fancy name!'

'She found it in an old "Ossian," and thought it so combined Sarah and Mary, that she insisted on our all calling her so.'

'Did she get her brothers to do so?'

Aurelia laughed, but observed that we must not betray such an absurd fancy; and indeed she had never let me disclose her own peculiar Christian name, and never openly called me anything but Miss Lipscombe, till I quite longed for once to hear the sound of Effie.

I had that pleasure soon. We two were sent to the station to meet the new-comer, and the first greeting was a happy shriek of 'Effie! dear Effie! dearest Aurelia! how sweet of you!'

I don't know whether I should have known her; for the girl who used to be all legs and arms and hair, untidy and boisterous, was now tall and elegant, and fashionably dressed, though still warm and impetuous, as she rushed up to kiss both of us; and I know Aurelia winced, as she thought of the porters.

Her luggage went in the omnibus, and we walked together, telling her the names of the streets, and answering her inquiries about the Robinsons, explaining how they consisted of the Doctor, his wife, the two grown-up sons of the first marriage, and the four or five little ones of the second. Just as Sally's inquiries were becoming more individual, the prudent Aurelia chose to ask after Mrs. Shilling, as if anything ever were the matter with her!

'Very well, and absorbed in cares as usual! Ah! you have one another, you happy girls! You cannot have known what it is to meet no sympathy or attention when one most needs it.'

Here comes the melancholy position, thought I; and I put a leading question, hoping there was nothing amiss.

'Oh no, not to a casual observer! But though it

was all very well when we were little, mamma would be much better advised to cease to have inmates. Curates are human, though they be vowed to celibacy.'

'Are they?' said the Grey Mouse.

'Everyone knows that Mr. Shelburne is. I don't mind telling you, dearest darlings, for I know it safe with you; but I fear the mischief is irreparable, and I am sure it wasn't my fault.'

'What!' I cried, in spite of a poke from the unfeeling Aurelia's parasol; 'did you refuse him?'

'No! Poor man! I did not let it come to that, but I refused the "Appendix to Hymns Ancient and Modern;" and I saw he could hardly command his countenance, for he was forced to bite his lip. When mamma told me to mend his hood when it caught on a nail in the vestry, she little thought of the consequences; and I never could open her eyes, though even Jack used to chaff about it.'

'Mr. Shilling chaffed?' said Aurelia.

'Yes, as if he thought it serious! I was quite thankful to be leaving home. It is enough to reconcile me to the painful present.'

I began to protest that she would be very happy; but she shook her head pathetically, and said, 'At the best, a governess's is a trying position.'

I don't think she was *very* unhappy, after all.

She was a winning creature, with the family high spirits; the little girls were charmed with her, and so was their mother; but she said Dr. Robinson scrupulously avoided her, and was civil by rule and measure, and that the man-servant always looked at her with a covert sneer, while the maids offered her as many slights as they durst. I thought it very odd that the Robinson servants should be so unlike those we lived with: but once when I said so to Aurelia, she answered, '*C'est selon les règles!*'

Indeed, she soon drove Selma out of all patience by her cold caution; and in fact they were seldom alone together, and Wilfred's presence hushed all confidences.

Now Mr. Nutley's house stood on the road most convenient for walks, and Selma timed her promenades so as to meet us coming out for ours, an arrangement which did not please my trio; for they were between fifteen and twelve, and did not want to be encumbered day after day with little Katie and Laura Robinson. Ellen had a passion for ferns, and Alice for grasses, and they wanted to collect and discuss them with me, so that they much disliked to have me engrossed by Miss Shilling; while I was hearing of her dread of a letter from the celibate curate: though he never wrote, he only went to spend a month in Switzerland—we alone knew why!

A hint from Mrs. Nutley made me aware that I must give up these walks; but we still had a good deal of time together on Saturdays and Sundays, not interrupted by the parish matters that came to the Vicar's wife, and in which Aurelia had volunteered her assistance. Selma was a much more interesting companion than poor Aurelia, and we used to discuss our pupils' characters together, and laugh over their mistakes or naughtinesses. I knew when Laura was put into a corner and began to sing 'Begone dull care,' and how her papa had wickedly laughed and taken her out; and I told anecdotes of Frances's incredible turn for mis-spelling; but I had nothing to communicate comparable to Selma's knowledge of the aspects of Dr. Robinson's patients (for she could see the front gate from her bedroom window), nor to her description of his temper at breakfast, when she was certain that he was being hard on his sons, and that dear Mrs. Robinson was trying to excuse them. Another time she found out, by the sharp ringing of the dining-room bell, that they had had a great dispute, and that it must have been on economy: for Mrs. Robinson bought a new bonnet at Fairleigh, though she had been talking over London bonnet-shops only a week before. It was evidently a sacrifice; but dear Mrs. Robinson thought nothing of such things when family peace was at stake.

However, Selma's feelings were a good deal injured by her Christmas holidays being fixed to begin and end just after the young Robinsons' vacation. She thought the motive transparent, and that it need not have so openly been shown that a poor governess was out of the pale of humanity; but we viewed her as lucky, since neither of us had any holidays. Poor Aurelia had had no home since Bryan's mother had died; and though she was asked to go home with Selma, Wilfred was so unwell that she would not leave him. My journey to York was too costly to be made more than once a year; and as Bryan was laying down a railroad in Wallachia, I should not have seen him even if I had gone to my brother's.

Selma was so free with her confidences, and so anxious for mine, that I had allowed her to know of my engagement; but I never told her Bryan's name, for after keeping it for three years from my kind friends, I could not let it come round to them through Sally Shilling; and I began to perceive that it would certainly do so, for I was much annoyed by finding that she had told Miss Leeson, the organist's daughter, that Alice had no ear, and that I much regretted Ellen's being allowed to read 'Lorna Doone' rather than 'Guy Mannering.' I trembled for a week, lest it should come round to Mrs. Nutley that I had found fault, but I heard no more of it.

In the spring, the scarlatina broke out in Fairleigh, and Mr. and Mrs. Nutley had such a dread of it, that we were all carried off to Dieppe without loss of time and settled in lodgings there. Mr. Nutley went home to his business at the bank, to his wife's great anxiety. He escaped; but it was a very severe visitation in the town, and went through both the Halstead and Robinson families. Selma had it slightly, but Aurelia nursed both her children through it while their mother was ill; and Dr. Robinson said that she saved little Wilfred's life. Afterwards, both families went to Clackmouth for sea air; and when Selma had thus been disinfected, she went home. We only heard all this from Mr. Nutley, for all letters from infected houses were forbidden.

We, meantime, travelled about, seeing Churches, Cathedrals, and wonderful old towns in Normandy and Brittany, as soon as Mr. Nutley had time to join us; and on our return my visit to my brother was to begin. It was very kind of the Nutleys to give me the opportunity of seeing so much, but they said they wanted me as interpreter, for certainly their French was funny. I found Mr. Nutley describing himself one day as *banqueroute*, instead of *banquier*; and he always said '*ça ira*,' when he meant 'that will do.' The worst of it was, that I never knew where to tell Bryan to write to me.

R

We were to cross to Dover, and according to Mrs. Shilling's kind standing invitation, I wrote to ask to spend a night at her house before starting for York. I received one of Selma's affectionate outpourings, declaring that she had an immense deal to tell me, but she was going out with Dick, and could only tell me she had found the *him* of all her life! She felt it.

When, tired and battered after my crossing, and yearning for a letter from Bryan, I arrived at the kindly door on that sultry summer evening, I found all the party in the down-stair rooms doubly radiant, and I had not taken off my hat before I heard the cause. It was not Selma's engagement to '*him*,' as I expected, but a legacy, which added fifty pounds a year to Mrs. Shilling's little income. Moreover, Jack had been taken into the firm as a partner, Dick had got a situation as house-surgeon at a county hospital, Jem had achieved a scholarship, and the whole family were beaming with good-nature and prosperity.

They would not let me mount the many stairs before regaling me with their little feast, including penny ices—over which how we talked! all sorts of scraps of news flying about, and drolleries flying between the boys, while Mrs. Shilling's round full voice merrily scolded them for their nonsense, and declared poor Mr. Shelburne would not be able to write his sermon.

I saw Selma trying to look pensive, and concluded that *he* was not Mr. Shelburne; but I had not long finished the meal before Mrs. Shilling said I was too much tired to laugh any more, and she herself took me up to the room I was to share with Sally, and left us with strict injunctions not to talk all night. Would that we had obeyed her!

I began by asking after the Halsteads. Wilfred was much better, and seemed likely to improve in health; but Agnes's was a very slow recovery, and it was feared she would become delicate. 'So I saw hardly anything of Aurelia at Clackmouth,' Selma said; 'she was wrapped up in those children. But there was her cousin.'

'What cousin?' I asked, thinking over the family.

'Mr. Arrowsmith. He knows you, he said so.'

'Is he in England?' I asked, amazed.

'He came back from Vienna a month ago, and was at Clackmouth superintending the suspension bridge. O Effie! such a noble-looking figure! such a picturesque head, with auburn hair and beard; he might be a model for Sir Lancelot, or Michel Angelo, or anybody—with the grace of a foreigner, and the dignity of an Englishman! He might be an Austrian prince. Oh! I am so happy! Such a distinguished name too—Bryan Maxwell Arrowsmith!'

I only remember sitting bolt upright, feeling dizzy

and sick, but desperate to hide all and hear the worst. I suppose I asked what right the wretched girl had to be so happy, for I know she answered, 'Every right that meeting hearts can give.'

Much was not wanting to make her run on: 'No, he had not spoken to her formally, he had given her to understand that he could not in honour; indeed from what Aurelia said, she was sure there was some unfortunate entanglement. What had Aurelia said? Just nothing, I might be sure, poor dear little Grey Mouse! but she had hinted that her cousin Bryan was engaged, and that it was nonsense to fancy anything, but she would tell no more; and of course it was some old master engineer's horrid daughter who had drawn him in.'

I must have said something about treachery to an old master engineer's horrid daughter; for the next thing I heard was, 'Of course not; but circumstances were strong, *would* be strong.' She should never forget that dreadful evening, when two horrible odious ruffians pursued her with loud shouts; and there he stood, like Amyas Leigh—like all that was chivalrous, and —yes, she must say it—encircled her waist with his arm, and told her there was nothing to fear; while they shrank daunted from his very look, scathed and blighted, while he pressed her half fainting to his heart. Ah! the thrill of those beating hearts would be with her for ever! He assisted her to the beach, placed her on a bench, called Aurelia, and attended on her like the very soul of chivalry.

And then there was the pic-nic! See! And deep in her dressing-box was the forget-me-not he had gathered for her, and with such a look I can't think how I kept my fingers from crushing the miserable little dried flower! And lastly there was his photograph—a new one I had never seen before, handsomer than ever; but what was that to me now?

I don't know how I could have borne it if Mrs. Shilling had not come back, insisting that we must not talk a moment longer, or I should be ill to-morrow, for I looked like a ghost; and she carried off her daughter to help Dick, who was raving for her to accompany him in practising for a concert.

I put myself to bed in haste, that Sally might think me asleep when she came back, though sleep was far enough off. Nothing was present with me but the one idea that Bryan only thought of me as a troublesome encumbrance, to whom he was bound in honour! I need not tell you the stunned misery of that night, nor how desolate it seemed to have to get up and go about the world—just as if one had to begin without any sun in the sky!

Mrs. Shilling thought I looked so poorly, that she hardly consented to my travelling, though I was desperate to get away; for that house was perfectly intolerable to me, and I thought there would be some relief in moving on. I only wished there was no arriving!

I could not speak of it to my brother and his wife; I could only tell them that Bryan was at Vienna when I heard last; and I acted cheerfulness with all my might, excitement giving me a little success for the first three days.

Then, one afternoon, as Mary and I were coming home, we heard a quick step behind us, and there was Bryan with his little bag over his shoulder! The first thing, after the old instinctive leap of my foolish heart, was the thought, 'Auburn hair and eyes, the traitor's complexion.' I was proud; I recollected the photograph and forget-me-not, and steeled myself. I would be generous. One heart was enough for him to break!

He followed us into the drawing-room, and Mary left us together. I tried to follow her, but he caught me, saying he could not spare me to take off my things, for he had to go on by the next train to Glasgow, but he had stolen this hour to tell me he had hopes of an excellent appointment.

'Had you not better tell Miss Shilling?' I coldly said.

I remember his wondering eyes; but the wrath I

had nursed for a fortnight was too hot not to break forth. I told him, though my throat seemed bursting, that I knew what his professions were worth; I knew how he liked to play with his attentions, and count hearts as savages count heads. He pleaded something about noticing a nice girl as my friend. I said that was a fine excuse; I knew how far he had gone, and what expectations he had raised.

'You don't mean,' he said, 'that the girl is fool enough to talk of expectations!'

'Making fools of poor women is such a favourite pastime, that I will not indulge you with hearing,' I said.

Then he grew displeased. He said if this were only a little jealous petulance, it was hard to waste this single hour on it; and as I repeated the words in intense disgust, he gravely demanded whether I seriously distrusted him.

'How could I help it?' I said.

Then he answered that if so, he was of my mind, that all must be at an end between us, for there could be no love where there was no trust in a man's word and honour.

I would not look round: the cab came for him at the moment, and he was gone.

O Lucy! the wretchedness of it! Resentment and fancied generosity to Selma bore me up a little, and so did the great anger of George and Mary, who thought me ridiculous beyond conception. George had been hearing accounts of Bryan's ability and power of resource, which made him declare that by my own abominable folly and jealousy I had thrown away fame, fortune, baronetcies, and I can't tell what; while Mary lectured me on the folly of heeding what a man said to a pretty girl in one's absence. It was very horrid, but the strife helped to bear me up; and I never gave way except at night; and even then, except at the very worst, there was a sort of savage comfort in thinking of my grand sacrifice, and imagining myself listening to scales, while Selma was being presented at court! For I had opened the way of happiness to both; for it was plain that Byran was glad to be released, or he would have sought reconciliation; but as the lingering hope died out, and I ceased to start at every knock, I was convinced that he had carried out his inconstancy.

I was glad to get back where no one but Aurelia knew anything, and I braced myself to hear of Selma's engagement; but I would not go to Mrs. Shilling's on the way, and made only one long day's journey. Mrs. Nutley saw I was very tired, and would not let my dear girls hang about me long, but sent me to my room, where I think I had my first good night's rest for weeks. Everybody said my holiday had done me little good, and the next day Mrs. Nutley seriously asked after my health. Presently she said that she wished to put me on my guard, for she feared Miss Shilling was a great talker; Mrs. Robinson had been annoyed at finding that all her family affairs were discussed at the organist's, and she would have parted with Miss Shilling but that the children were so fond of her, and she was so nice with them. Mrs. Nutley did not blame me, as I knew in my secret soul I deserved; she only gave me a caution.

She thought me too much tired to go out with the children, and bade me lie down, bringing me the most interesting books in her box. Alas! I could only think of the change since I last had been in that school-room.

By-and-by there was a knock: Selma, tender and kind as ever, and greatly grieved to find me poorly, but brimful of confidences. I shut my eyes and turned my head away, to be able to bear it; but behold, it was to consult her only sympathising friend on the painful subject of Edward Robinson's manifest attentions; and the evident annoyance that they caused his stepmother, whose manner had become quite altered.

'Are you sure that is the reason?' I asked.

'Quite sure! It has been most distressingly marked ever since we came home. And Aurelia is so cold! If the Leesons were not a resource, I don't know what I should have done.'

I was in a mood to say something dissagreeable, so I observed, 'Are you sure it may not be the gossiping at the Leesons that she objects to?'

'I never gossip!' said Selma, with dignity. 'I thought you a friend, Euphemia Lipscombe; and this is the way you treat my confidence! Gossip, indeed! as if I ever gossipped!'

I did not go on then, I was too sick and faint of heart. I longed to see Aurelia again, but she did not come to me; we only shook hands coldly when we met in society.

At last, I felt so unutterably miserable and lonely, that one day when we had chanced to meet in the lane, I said, 'O Aurelia, do not cast me off too!'

'I am sorry,' she said, in a hesitating way.

And then I broke out, asking her why she had never written to me, nor warned me when Bryan's heart was being stolen away from me before her very eyes. I was so unhappy, that I knew not what I said. She listened, and I believe all she said was 'Poor Effie!' and once she asked me what made me think his heart was gone. I told her all Selma had said, and asked what I could gather from it. To which she answered, 'Selma!!!'

The next afternoon—it was Saturday—there came

into my school-room Aurelia and Selma, the latter looking rather like a little spaniel led in a string. Aurelia gravely said, 'Sarah, I should be obliged if you would explain to Effie Lipscombe your reasons for claiming my cousin, Bryan Arrowsmith, as your admirer.'

I began something desperate and incoherent about no use and never minding; but Aurelia looked stern. 'I do mind,' she said. 'I demand that justice should be done to my cousin! I wish to know what grounds Sarah has for announcing that he was paying her attention.'

'Don't talk of it in that dreadful formal way!' cried poor Selma, beginning to cry; while I broke out with 'No, Aurelia, let her alone. She has the proofs—the flower, the photograph.'

'When did he give you the flower?' said Aurelia.

'The day—the day of the pic-nic at the castle,' said Selma. And at a stern 'Well!' 'He climbed down into the moat, and pulled up a whole armful of water-plants, and said, "Here's a contribution for the ladies!" and you pulled out a flowering rush, and I a forget-me-not. But he really gave it.'

'And the photograph? How many more did he distribute?' asked Aurelia.

'Five or six,' faintly said Selma. 'We all had them.'

Aurelia looked so judicial, that she withheld my outcry, and made Selma go on to the catastrophe in the lane. It sounded very different now. Selma had been frightened, and had flown up to Bryan and caught his arm, being really agitated enough to need support to a seat. Aurelia here contributed what his summons to herself had been. 'I say, Relia, do come to this girl, or she will go into fits on my hands about two navvies who were minding their own business.'

And when I vehemently demanded how she could have made such representations to me, she looked down and declared I had taken it too seriously. 'One always does fancy things,' she said.

'I hope only *one* does, not two,' I said; 'and if fancied, they should go no further.'

'Oh; but it would be so stupid! There would be no interest in life.'

There it dawned on her that it was my happiness that had been sacrificed to making life interesting to her; and she was despairing and furious, reproaching Aurelia for not telling her; and when Aurelia reminded her of the warning, she said there was a great difference between a tiresome abstraction of a stranger and her own dear darling Effie; nor could she see that it would have been equally wrong in Bryan to desert the abstraction of a stranger. Indeed, she went off, firmly believing it was all the fault of

Aurelia's unkind silence, and much aggrieved that I could not be persuaded to say so, since Aurelia had had no permission to speak ; and in fact, there had been no flirtation at all on Bryan's part, while, as to Selma, I must do her the justice to say that however she might dwell in imagination and in confidence on ordinary little civilities, her manner was never amiss ; and I don't believe that either the celibate, or Edward Robinson, or Bryan, or the organist, ever suspected that she was breaking their hearts.

She was a warm-hearted creature, and hung so pathetically about me, that I had more comfort in her than in Aurelia, who, though she had caused justice to be done to her cousin, could not overlook my accepting Selma's rhapsodies *versus* his honour and word. The dismal days went on : I tried to work, but everything—music, lessons, and all—seemed to be one weary whirl in my head, and my one thought, sleeping and waking, was of my baseness in distrusting him for a moment, when he had trusted me so wholly.

Then came a Sunday morning : Selma rushed in full of horror to tell me that Mr. Arrowsmith had an appointment to lay down a railroad in Guinea. She knew it, for it was for the firm for which John worked, high pay and certain death ! She had done it—she knew she had, and she wanted my forgiveness.

I knew I had done it. My heart seemed dead

within me, yet I put on my bonnet and went to Church, but the pestilential air of Africa seemed closing round and stifling me and the insects buzzing in my ears, and once I thought I heard Bryan's voice in the surging tones behind me. Then I knew I was growing faint, for people were looking at me; and I thought I had better get out while I could. I couldn't, though. Pillars and arches and all seemed reeling and sinking into the crypt. Then I found myself with the fresh wind blowing on me, and the words in my ears through the buzz—'Poor dear child, it was all chatter!' 'It has half killed her, though.' Then came Dr. Robinson's voice, 'You have the remedy, I see; come, Miss Shilling.'

Yes, there I was, on a flat tombstone, with my head on Bryan's shoulder, and Aurelia keeping guard, and it was as if we had never parted.

'And we never will!' said Bryan.

'Never!' I said. I had rather have been under that tombstone at once than have had any more such tossings.

Bryan had been telegraphed for to London on Friday—had accepted the appointment, been busy all Saturday, and had come down by the early train. For he had found a card at the office with the words, 'Pure gossip; Come back. A. C. S.'

He begged Mrs. Nutley to forgive him for his

sudden robbery of her: but he had only a month in which to prepare, and he could not go without me. She was very kind, but she said, 'How could I get an outfit in the time?'

'One doesn't want much outfit for Guinea,' I said.

'My dear Effie, should I ever have dreamt of taking you there?'

And then it turned out that he was to arrange telegraphic communications between Guiana and the islands, and our home for the present is to be beautiful Trinidad.

So that was the history of my trouble. Dear Aurelia and Selma, they were both my bridesmaids, and both were equally happy. Selma says she has learnt a lesson for life; but she talks so much about it, that Aurelia evidently doubts her; yet I think there will be a little more watch on that eager tongue of hers when it breaks into confidences.

Bryan gave each a locket, and only my strongest representations hindered him from making one golden, the other silver. But Selma says that hers will always warn her that 'Least said is soonest mended.'

And so no more from
Your loving and happy
EUPHEMIA ARROWSMITH.

OUR GHOST AT FANTFORD.

OUR GHOST AT FANTFORD.

A DELIGHTED damsel was I, Fanny Fanshaw, when my brother Frank proposed to take me, some thirty years ago, to spend six weeks at Fantford Rectory.

It was his first experience in pastoral life, for he was at that time a tutor at Oxford. Our family home was in London, and our summer vacations were spent either abroad or by the sea-side, so that we knew little of country life.

Frank's friend, Harry Vaughan, was to be married, and during his wedding trip, my brother undertook to fill his place during his absence. Frank was assured, to his great relief, that, as it was near harvest-time, he need not trouble himself about the school; and as he felt that he must have a sister as a companion, I, the youngest of the family, was told off to accompany him.

Fantford was as far from everything as it is possible for any place to be within the limits of our island, and the natives were reported to be charmingly unspoilt and unsophisticated.

My notions of it were a mixture of the village in 'The Old Curiosity Shop,' where little Nelly died, and of a German toy box, peopled by the children in reward books.

I knew the parsonage was overgrown with roses, and felt as if I were going to spend six weeks in Dreamland.

We had a long journey by train, and one that seemed twice as long by a fly. Quite in the twilight of the long summer day, at the very bottom of a pit, between two hills, we saw a square tower of a church. Fantford at last!

'To the rectory,' we said, in our joy.

We turned in at a sweep-gate, and stopped at an ivied porch. There was great excitement; shouts of 'Johnny, Johnny!' girls rushed out with flying locks; boys rushed in with flags; a beaming mother came forward; then all stood still, with blank looks.

'I beg your pardon,' said Frank. 'There is some mistake. Is not this Fantford?'

'Fantford St. Magnus.'

'Fantford St. Agnes—exactly so. Would you kindly direct us to the rectory? I am come to take your rector's place during his wedding tour,' said Frank.

There was a stifled explosion among the young people, and the lady's eyes twinkled merrily as she gravely said, 'The rector of Fantford St. Magnus went on his wedding tour fifteen years ago, and I went with him. It is Fantford St. Agnes you are looking for. Mr. Fanshaw, I think.'

I don't know which was worst, our confusion at our blunder, or our despair at the miles we had to retrace before we could get to the right turn.

However, the hospitable woman would not let us go till she had recruited us with tea from her comfortable board, to which her rector presently returned; and we found that Mr. Vaughan had specially recommended us to their good offices. Indeed, they were so friendly that we did not start till late.

There was not much darkness that summer night, but the way was an endless winding in and out of lanes, up and down, and when we did get to the right rectory, and heard the welcome sound of ground under our wheels, every window was dark, and we knocked and rang in vain. At last a window was thrown up, and a voice shouted:

'Be it Jem Richards, up to the George?'

'Aye, sure enough! Get up, can't you?'

'And ye're not the ghost of the coach and horses?'

'Not as I knows on, you great numbskull! Come and let in the parson and the lady!'

'Coming!' responded from within, while I whispered my raptures at being taken for a ghost, and Frank replied by grunts, as if the personation of one.

By this time, a shock-headed lad was opening the door. Behind it a tidy old housekeeper body welcomed us with a hundred excuses for having given us up and gone to bed, when a reasonable time had past since the last train at the distant station.

We had supped so well that we went off at once to our beds, I trying on the way to extract the legend of the coach and horses. But Mrs. Thorpe held herself superior to such folly, saying that—

'Will Owselbird was a very ignorant man, but she had made him sleep in the back kitchen because it always "made her creep to think of what might happen without no man in the house." Coach and horses! No, I need not be afraid. She never saw it nor heard it. If I was nervous, she would come and sleep in my room.'

The more I tried to persuade her that I was only curious, not alarmed, the more she tried to reassure me by protests against my superstition, till at last I bade her good-night, intending to resume my researches for the coach and horses on the Monday.

I may as well say that it always did elude me. Nobody in broad daylight would allow before a young lady from London, that there was any such thing. Will Owselbird looked stolid and silent over the pigsty when he was questioned, and only the great commotion respecting *the* ghost, elicited that everyone had 'heerd tell' that a coach and six was wont to drive up the street at midnight, and was always a sign for death. Our fly was certainly a mitigated form of it.

Daylight showed me a cozy room, and a lovely view of a rocky river, pasture and hill; but, alas, all the roses I had hoped to see, and other creepers, were sprawling uncomfortably over the path, or tied back, while the house was being new 'painted,' to keep it weather-tight. The first of the country's 'odorous sweet' that met my enthusiastic nostrils was the smell of paint mixed with varnish.

Good old Mrs. Thorpe was full of apologies, and had made superhuman efforts to get three rooms habitable; but the rest of the house was full of poles, and pails of whitewash, and pots of paint, left there by faithless workmen, who ought to have finished their work a week before.

On our second Sunday at Fantford there was a funeral. One of the numerous Owselbirds had died in the county hospital, and his body had been sent home for burial.

The poor wife and children cried most bitterly all the time of the service, and but that we saw them surrounded with Owselbirds of all ages, we should have gone home with them to endeavour to comfort them.

When we went to condole the next day, we found a stout girl turning a mangle, and the widow folding vigorously, though she paused at once, and in the midst, burst forth into floods of tears, while she told us what a turn her poor husband's death had given her, coming so unexpected.

'It was,' she said, 'an attachment such as he had had often before.' ('Rather a startling communication for a wife,' thought I, but she went on.) 'He was always having them attachments, and then he couldn't do no good, not for a week at a time. Bilious attachments they were, so old Granny Owselbird said! but Dr. Elsted—he's a feeling man, is Dr. Elsted—"John my poor man," says he, "they'll do you more good up to the hospital than I can, for you'll be dieted there."

'And John, he was set upon it, so Mr. Vaughan gets an order just before he went away, and sent him in George Owselbird's market-cart, little thinking how it would turn out.

'And yet my mind misgave me, for there was a little robin come flapping its wings, that very morning and pecking at the window, as if 'twas for somebody. And then a-Thursday comes a paper to say there had been a information, and my poor man, he were gone like the grass of the field.'

We had reason to believe the fatal information was inflammation, but the suddenness of his death had astonished everyone. John Owselbird had, it seemed, always been sickly and ailing, seldom able for much work, and chiefly maintained by his wife's exertions as washerwoman. So she did not seem to need assistance so much as sympathy, and this she had in plenty, for her poor John was, the public voice said, 'a chap as kept himself to his self, and was so steady he was like to fall asleep standing, and never had words with no one. A quiet man was John Owselbird,' was always the climax of his praise.

We spent as much time out of doors in the lovely country as we could, and when at home, chiefly sat in the shade of a large plane-tree, where we luxuriated with our books and drawing.

There we were one evening, when with a tread like a charge of horse, hair flying, eyes starting out of her head, in upon us rushed a great girl, sobbing and panting out something about 'Father!'

'Is your father ill?' asked Frank.

She stretched out her hand and uttered, 'No! No, sir, but them as buries 'em can lay 'em.'

She began shuddering and crying, and perceiving

by this time that she was the daughter of the newly-made widow, we made her swallow some tea, and she brought out the words,—

'Father's comed again.'

'Nonsense!' cried Frank.

And as the poor girl shivered and cried, and was obviously frightened out of her wits, he began assuring her that it was some fancy or some trick. But the girl stuck to it that her father's ghost had really looked at her from his own house door, when she came home from gleaning.

She had rushed back to her mother, who at first told her not to be such a gawk as to make her believe such a story as that. The mother had, however, looked in at the cottage window, seen the apparition, and 'now,' said poor Betsy, 'she be in at Tailor Owselbird's, in the screaming asterisks, so strong that it takes two of 'em to hold her.'

'I suppose I must come down, at any rate,' said Frank, getting up.

'There must be something in it,' said I.

'Either some effect of light in the window, or, what might be worse, a tramp in the house,' said Frank.

Just as I was feeling a little balked, the gate clicked, and in came the parish clerk, David Cambridge, a fine old man, with a beautiful head, and reverent, apostolic air, and a gentle simplicity of manner that I never saw surpassed in any station.

He was reckoned 'a fine scholar,' and being a sensible man, was an oracle with his neighbours, and our great counsellor in parish matters. He had the key of the church in his hand, and touching his hat, demanded,—

'If you please, sir, shall you not want the surplice and the great church Bible to exercise the wandering spirit of John Owselbird, deceased?'

'I must see him first, Master Cambridge! What! do you believe in him, too?'

'There ain't no manner of doubt about it, sir,' so quoth the clerk, to my mingled terror and satisfaction. 'He have been seen by a many, a flitting up the road with just his stumbling manner of gait. A knock-kneed chap always was Jock Owselbird, poor fellow; and by what they tells me, there's good cause as he shouldn't rest in his grave—not without you exercises your office, your reverence, and exercises him.'

'He seems to be exercising himself without my assistance,' muttered my brother; but I, struck with pleasurable awe and excitement, began,—

'But you will exorcise him.'

'We shall see.'

'You know you must get a license from the Bishop.'

'And let the ghost walk all the time?'

'Don't you remember that authentic case where the woman's ghost used to meet the boy going to school, till he told the clergyman, who drew a pentacle, and interrogated her? Can you draw a pentacle, Frank?'

'With the assistance of a pair of compasses.'

There was something incredulous in Frank's tone, that made me doubtful whether he were worthy of an encounter with a live ghost. We set forth, my trepidation growing on me so much, as we saw the reality of the commotion, that I began to doubt whether the appearance of an undoubted ghost were so great a treat as I had fancied in the abstract. But then, what a distinction it would be to have seen it!

Every cottage had a woman at its door, all standing out to see the parson going to lay the ghost, and each looking so awestruck that my heart beat faster and faster.

One woman—sister, as we understood, to the deceased—joined us, with her apron to her eyes, crying and sobbing, but evidently enjoying the melancholy distinction. Presently, however, she darted forward, exclaiming:

'That's he! That's he as has done what is a hindering of my poor brother from lying quiet in his grave! Don't be after hiding of yourself.'

'Speak up, Jabez Mortlock,' added the clerk, 'and it will be the better for you.'

Jabez Mortlock, the very big man who usually predominated over the cheese, bacon, and candles in the village shop, had assumed a wonderful yellow lividness of complexion, and with his corduroy knees knocking together, and his knuckles up to his eyes, like a naughty boy, sobbed out:

'Don't ye make me come and see him, sir, don't ye now, and I'll tell you all.'

Then coming up close, he uttered, in what was meant for a whisper. 'Tell him not to come after that 'ere pig no more, for his wife shall have the full value of it, and you and Master Cambridge shall be the judges, sir. Tell him I would not have done it, if I'd known it would have preyed on him like this, but a poor man like me can't afford no bad debts, sir, and when he was took off to the hospital, there seemed no other way but fur to take the pig. 'Tis sold, sir, but I'd try to get it back at a loss, if it would be more agreeable, or Betsy could take it out in groceries. Anything not to have him haunting of me like this;' and he began to cry again.

'He ain't used to it, ain't Jabez,' chimed in a tall, tough, wiry dame, who looked as if she had enforced her husband's seizure of the pig for his debt.

'Have you seen this?' demanded Frank.

The man's whole bulk shuddered. The woman said, 'O yes, sir. Jabez was just bringing in the lamps, and I was serving little Polly Smart with a quarter of a pound of lard, when we both seen his face as white as miss's gownd there, looking over the half door. We up and ran out at the back in one moment, and there's the child still in under the counter and won't come out. It will be well if Jabez ever gets the better of the turn.'

'Well,' said Frank, oracularly; 'if your conscience reproaches you with having been hard on the distressed family, you had better make full restitution.'

And as we moved on, followed at a respectful distance by the whole population, my brother observed:

'I understand it now. It is a figment of this Mortlock's uneasy conscience which has infected the rest of the parish.'

I don't know whether I was relieved or disappointed.

We crossed the village green—Frank and I, supported by the valiant David Cambridge grasping the church key, poor Mrs. Owselbird and her daughters emerging from a neighbour's cottage to observe us a little in the rear, and a crowd behind.

Manfully we advanced up the path, but I suspect Frank's heart was as near his mouth as mine when in the darkening twilight of the cottage room, we actually did see a white, lank, shadowy form bending over the hearth. I think we all started back, but Frank rallied first.

Is it the man?' he whispered to the Clerk.

O yes, sir, not a doubt of it,' in an awestruck whisper.

'John Owselbird, is it you?' said Frank at the door, with great resolution, and only a very faint quiver.

'Yes, sure,' was the answer, in a weak, frail tone.

'What brings you here?' demanded Frank, still more solemnly.

'George Owselbird's cart, sir. He set me down at the bottom o' the lane. I thought they'd be glad to see me, but they be all runned away.'

'Why, my good man, no wonder. Didn't we bury you on Sunday?'

At that moment, a pony carriage pulled up at the door, and the cheery voice of the neighbour clergyman was heard exclaiming:

'Is Mr. Fanshaw there? Why, Mr. Fanshaw, what have you been doing? Burying one of my flock, have you?'

'Aye, aye,' quoth our *revenant*. 'That's the way of it. It was poor John Owselbird of Fantford St. Magnus as is dead, and they must have sent him home instead of me. I had no time to let my missus know I was discharged, for there's a fever broke out in the hospital, and they wanted to clear their wards of all as could go out. So that's where it is.'

Then we shouted for the woman to come in and attend on her husband, for he looked thin and exhausted enough soon to become a ghost in good earnest, if not fed and warmed.

'But bless me,' cried she, while we were administering some port wine we had sent for from the rectory. 'Whatever shall I do with my beautiful suit of weeds?'

The rector of Fantford St. Agnes instantly purchased them at a liberal valuation, as a consolation to the right widow—whose husband, we heard, had been a sad ne'er-do-weel.

Jabez Mortlock could not for very shame retract his promise about the pig, and Betsy had the price out in groceries at different times; but I am afraid he drove very hard bargains with her, and that poor John in the flesh was not nearly so effective a protector as his disembodied self.

ANNA'S WEDDING CAKE.

'I'LL give the cake,' said my Aunt Susan. 'You write and order it, Susie.'

I was the one told off from the rest of the family to attend upon Aunt Susan, who lived in 'the Dower House,' about a mile from our merry home in the vicarage.

I was her god-daughter, and so I had, as I used to tell the rest, to do all the work of a companion, not for money, but——

Well, it would have been better for us both if it had been more for love. And as Anna used to tell me when she lectured me, it was hardly fair to say it was not for money, for Aunt Susan did give me more pocket-money than any of the others had, and such lovely bonnets and good silk dresses that I was sometimes quite ashamed of going out in them, when my sisters were only in serge— with home-made imitations of my bonnets upon their heads.

I would have given them all my finery to have shared their merry evenings of fun and frolic, and their glorious expeditions. I know now that Aunt

Susan meant to be very kind, and spared me often to her own inconvenience; and mamma, Anna and Emily used to change places with me, whenever they could. However, it used to seem to me that I was at home just enough to be tantalized by hearing of all that was delightful, in which I could not share.

Of course, I felt it all the more all that summer when George Barton was hanging about at the vicarage, and more pleasant things happened than ever, while Anna never did come as of old to read to my aunt and write her letters.

For poor Aunt Susan had a cataract coming, and was entirely dependent on one of her great-nieces for eyes. She was very much delighted when Anna accepted George Barton, because she had known his father in old times, and when the wedding-day was fixed, she declared that she would give the cake, and that I must write for it to Gunter's, without delay; since George had to go out as acting partner to Smyrna, and there was no time to lose.

'Let it be a really handsome cake,' said my aunt, 'big enough to cut up and distribute all round. In my time, no one thought of sending wedding-cards without a good wedge of the cake in a three-cornered box, and there were always two cards tied up with white satin ribbon and silver twist.'

'But that would be thought vulgar now, aunt.'

'Vulgar, indeed! As if I had not helped to direct the cards when all the Ladies St. Piers were married. Then they came to omitting the cake, then to having both names together on one card, and sending them by the penny-post,' (I wish I could render the disgust with which Aunt Susan uttered the words, penny-post,) 'and now they would put you off with "No cards" at the end of the notice in the newspaper. No, no; Anna shall have a proper cake to cut up for her friends, and you write at once for it.'

'How large shall I say, Aunt Susan?' I asked, after writing the date, and "Mrs. Railston requests Messrs. Gunter"——

'How large? Let me see. My cake was about as big round as a bandbox, and it had a temple with two little doves upon the top of it.'

'One can't say as big as a bandbox,' I said, doubtfully. 'How big is a bandbox?'

'You had better measure.'

So I got my ribbon-yard, found a bandbox, and measured.

It was—speaking roundly—a yard and a half in girth. Aunt Susan said that would do very well.

I wrote her order with patience and minuteness, for which I highly commended myself, and then—as my father had promised to look in on her that afternoon—I ran, rather than walked, all the way home, to discuss with Emily the bridemaids' dresses, and hear all her recent discoveries on the manners and customs of people in love.

The next day, when I came home from an errand in the village, I found my poor aunt very much flustered by a yellow telegram envelope, which had just been brought in.

The boy was waiting to take back an answer, and she did not like to ask one of the servants to open it, being fully persuaded that it was something dreadful about that good-for-nothing Philip, who was always tormenting her.

'What is it, my dear child? Shall I send for your father? Don't be afraid to tell me. Let me hear at once.'

'What's this?' said I, puzzling out the rough writing. "Are the dimensions of the cake correct?"'

'Correct? What did you say, my dear?'

'A yard and a half, as you told me! How can they be so stupid? I had better write "Yes," I suppose, at once, or "All right."'

And all the evening, in the intervals of reading, Aunt Susan bewailed the degeneracy of the age that thought a yard and a half an excessive size for a wedding-cake.

Preparations went on, and we did not think much

more about this order till a day or two before the wedding, when the bill came by post, with the information that our esteemed order had been executed, and it was hoped would give satisfaction.

Such a bill it was, too! I was quite afraid to read the amount to Aunt Susan; and then we agreed either that London prices were fearfully exorbitant, or that there must be some mistake, about which I must write when the cake had arrived.

Worse and worse! The cake didn't come!

Everybody who went to the station was bidden to enquire for it; and the porters, guards, and every creature about the railway, must have been worn out with inquiries for the cake.

We were getting into an agony about it. On the very eve of the great day, we were at the vicarage, Aunt Susan and myself, she advising, and I helping in the setting up of the flowers, and we were considering whether the most rational person who could be spared should not be sent off to the nearest town to get the best ready-made cake it could offer, or whether by any violent effort, the supplementary cake that had been provided for the village people could be iced up, and an old ornament, kept under a glass case by the chief farmer's wife from her own wedding, could be borrowed. In the midst there arrived the bridegroom and his best man, who were to sleep at the Dower House; and as soon as the greetings were over, in the midst of whole baskets of flowers and pots of hot-house plants standing wildly about the entry, just as George was to be dragged in to see the trophy of wedding presents, he said:

'By-the-by, there's an enormous thing waiting at the station. We couldn't get it into the dog-cart, and I said we'd tell you to send a cart for it.'

Further pressed, he said it looked more as if it might hold a table than anything else. So we fixed our hopes on its being a Japan work-table from the only connection of ours whose contribution had not yet come in; but George warned Anna that she would have to leave it behind; he could never think of paying the freight in the steamer.

The baker's empty return cart was bidden to call, and we waited on the tiptoe of expectation, only occasionally breathing a word about the cake, until, at last, wheels were heard.

Everybody rushed out, to cause the cart to bring its precious burden to the front door instead of the back.

There stood the little light cart, entirely filled up by a huge round box, which little Mary suggested might contain the great Pennard cheese, which was made of one morning's milk of seven hundred cows.

It was lifted safely down by the efforts of all the male kind who stood round, and without crushing anyone's toes.

The next thing was to look at the card upon it, and Anna was the first to read, '"From Gunter's." I declare, it's the cake, after all!'

Some said, 'Impossible!' and others—I was one—suggested that the box was so large in order to protect the ornaments.

Futile hope. Those tools that had done so much unpacking did their work, and there it stood, a solid monster wedding-cake, white and sparkling as the driven snow, crowned with a whole garden of temples, Cupids and doves, but——

If it could come in at our front door, it would be lucky. It was vain to think of getting it into the dining-room.

'Susan,' said my aunt, whose poor eyes, dim as they were, were dazzled by this mass of white, 'Susan,' said she, panting, 'what have you done?'

'I did as you told me,' said I, in self-defence.

'What?' was the general shout. 'What did you write?'

'I wrote what Aunt Susan told me. A yard and a half—yes, I said a yard and a half in di—— Oh!'

It came over me then I had written *diameter*, by

way of a fine word, when I really meant girth, or circumference, and so the cake was more than three times as large as it was meant to be.

I ran right away to the darkest closet in the house, and cried. If Aunt Susan had not been mercifulness itself, and if Anna had not actually shed tears, and besought George himself to insist, I should never have appeared at the wedding. It was a day of misery to me, but I believe my mistake was an immense diversion to everybody except my poor aunt and myself.

They set up that dreadful cake in the hall; it would not go any farther, and an innocent little cousin of ours seeing it there, asked—

'Is *that* their honeymoon?' thinking it had come down bodily.

We bridesmaids had to go out and hack at it, while the best man suggested sending for an ice-saw. And then, when boxes of it had been sent to everybody, and all the parish had been presented with enough to cause a pestilence, there was still an intolerable quantity left. As to dreaming on it, it was a nightmare to us all, and the vicarage was half poisoned with the smell.

Papa declared that his Confirmation class sat round the study sniffing the fragrance; and mamma said she expected that all the rats and mice in the country would meet and hold revels in her hall.

At last we were told that wedding cake was an excellent thing in small quantities for a long sea voyage; so we sent off the remnant of the mighty cake to one of the agencies for supplying poor emigrants with comforts, spiritual, mental, and bodily. Then we breathed freely again, but I never hear the word diameter without thinking of the horrors I suffered about Anna's wedding-cake.

AUTOBIOGRAPHY
OF
PATTY APPLECHEEKS.

AUTOBIOGRAPHY OF PATTY APPLE-CHEEKS.

AUTOBIOGRAPHY! Yes, that's the right word. It means one's self talking about one's self. I like a good long word. It is worthy of myself, and every one knows that I am of distinguished extraction, or why am I seated in the place of honour on Miss Martha's davenport, after a course of adventures, which will be found to prove how personal merit can overcome prejudice?

I have not been more than three or four years in my present shape, but my recollections go much farther back, to a very different life. Instead of being one of the lovely models on which those great awkward, restless creatures, women and girls, try to form themselves, I was then part of the trunk of a Quarendon apple-tree, covered by a rough, dark coating of bark, yet full of a life and energy I have never since known. How beautiful it was to wake up and feel the rush of sap in the Spring, to find the bullfinches busy seeking the worms in the buds, to hear the blackbirds singing on our branches, and then to cover every twig with crimson buds, and rosy white blossoms which fell off only to give place to little green apples. These grew and deepened till they became splendid fruit, of the deepest and most shining crimson, surpassing even the much admired tint of my own cheeks.

Then it was that I saw most of the two-legged creatures formed on my present pattern. The lesser ones used to flock round to gather the fruits we kindly let fall for them on the grass, eating, filling their pinafores, pelting one another, and sometimes climbing into the tree for the finest. We were sorry when the man came with the ladder, and cleared the branches, for though that was the merriest day of all, no one came near us after it for the whole Autumn, our leaves fell off, and we fell asleep.

We always waked on one night. I think they called it Twelfth Night, when lights and voices came out into the darkness, and all the noisiest of the two-legged creatures came round to drink our healths, to wassail the apple-trees, as they called it. They always began with us. The farmer, and a very big man was he, with his cheeks flaming in the light of the lantern, used to dip a great silver tankard into a bucket full of cider with roasted apples floating in it, and drink our health, then fling the rest of the liquor in the cup at the trunk, singing with the rest in full chorus:

Here's to thee, old apple-tree !
Hence thou mayst bud, and hence thou mayst blow,
And hence thou mayst bear apples enow,
Hats full, caps full,
Bushel, bushel sacks full,
And my pockets full, too ! Hurra !

The farmer always aimed just at the part of the stock that enfolded me, and hence, no doubt, I derive the peculiar strength and geniality of my constitution.

Those were merry days, and there were many of them. The children grew from toddling things to shouting, scrambling boys and girls, then to youths and maidens; some passed out of sight, the jolly stout farmer grew old and bent, and his son grew to his breadth, but then became old in his turn. Over and over again this happened, but still our blossoms were as fair and our fruit as large and ruddy as ever, though our trunk did begin to lean forward a good deal, our branches crooked themselves, and we felt the winter winds more painfully; indeed, our right main limb was torn off one stormy night in March, and yet our flowers were of as lovely a pink and white, our fruit, as red and as shapely as ever.

But a new master had come—one of the boys who had played under us. How I do hate ingratitude! He never wassailed us on Twelfth Night! Oh, no! he was going to a party, and the wassailing was all nonsense. We could not believe that we heard such words from one of the very children whom we had fed year after year! Alas! worse was to come. We saw him walking about with a smart fellow like himself, talking of laying out the grounds. 'And,' said he, 'this old Quarendon must come down. It's quite a desight.'

A desight! Think of that from a lad who had learnt to climb on our branches, had fondled our apples till their red skin shone with polish, and whose teeth had often met in their juicy flesh! A desight, indeed!

'You may have the old stock for the stubbing it up, Dick,' he called out to one of his men, who said, 'Thank ye, sir,' as readily as if he, too, had not gorged our fruit, whenever he had a chance!

Yes, he came with his axe, and his wedge, and his pick! If we had made such a noise about it as those poor soft-fleshed animals do, what an outcry there would have been, whereas we only gave one great shivering groan as we came crashing down. There was an end for us of blue sky and fostering sunshine, of fresh, still dew bathing our leaves, and winds dancing in our twigs, of birds singing in our boughs, bees humming in our flowers, and black and red butterflies clustering on our fruit. Over for us was the spring of life and joy in every vein! I've seen much of life since that, but I would give up everything for that feeling once more.

We were divided, too, for Dick's axe split us up, and, all dismembered, we were thrown into a barrow and driven away to a cottage door.

'See, mammy, what a fine blaze!' cried a little wretch of a boy, picking me up in his little arms, and he was just going to have thrown me into the fire, but a woman interposed. I always observe that the women have more sense than the men, no doubt because they are more like us!

'Don't, Dickie,' she said. 'Apple-wood is too good for burning. My sister's husband, that is good for nothing but to carve toys, sets great store by it.'

'All right, mother,' said Dick. 'It don't cost me nothing, and he is welcome to it, poor chap.'

I was then tossed into a dark place, a shed, I believe, where I was perched upon by cocks and hens, and run over by rats and mice, till one morning, when we were all tumbled into a cart, where we went bump, bump, along without seeing or hearing anything but the grating beneath us, till we stopped, and after a little while someone said:

'Thank ye, thank ye kindly, Dick. It is just what my man likes, is a bit of apple-wood. Those bits of stick will be ever so much to him.'

Here was appreciation again! My spirits rose, and ere long I began to awaken to my new, my present life, my true destiny. I was no longer a bit of a tree, or a mere log, but was shaped into a form of my own. It was to Dick's wife's sister's husband that I owe my figure, features, complexion. I cannot describe the process, but here is the result: My well-rounded head, and my body so conveniently tapered to a sharp point, were first formed, and then my complexion was added, pink with a deeper flush in the cheeks, two dots in my neat little nose, eyes black as sloes, looking confidently straight before me, without any of that winking nonsense which I hear has recently come in among dolls, and a smiling little mouth, ever benignant and complacent, as befits my never ruffled temper. My dark locks came, I believe, out of a mattress; my legs were rolls of calico; my arms, ready gloved in deep red, came from a store of such useful articles, and were nailed on to my shoulders. So charmed was the sister's husband with me that he called out, 'There, Polly, there's a regular Miss Applecheeks, ain't she?'

I wondered he did not touch up his own cheeks, as he had done by mine, for they were very thin and white, and his legs seemed like mine—for show, not vulgar things for use, for I never saw him stand upon them, but he always lay on a bed in the corner of the room. When he called, a woman in a white cap, with a face puckered up and ruddy-brown, like my old neighbours, the russet apples, in a frost, bustled up, and she was struck with me at once.

'Sweetly pretty, Jem, to be sure. Let her get dry, and I'll dress her in a bit of my old missus's curtains, that I've always kept for something out of the common. We ought to get something extra for she.'

So the good creature sewed me into a beautiful dress, a crimson, glazed ground, with large blue roses on a bush with yellow leaves. One rose was so large that it covered my whole lap, though my skirts stood out from my elegant taper waist as if I had worn crinoline.

I expected to be set up in the window to attract the passers-by, but I found myself again shut up in the dark, until one morning I was taken out and seated in a large, flat basket, comfortably lined for my reception, with a pincushion at my feet for my support, five or six lesser dolls to attend on me, three monkeys to leap over sticks for my amusement, and four black and white-spotted horses, of the peculiar breed intended for the use of dolls. It was plain that I was going forth to seek my fortune, fully equipped with my proper suite.

The sister's husband put the whole in order, and showed much care that I should be comfortable and not feel the jolts, and his wife seemed quite overpowered with the honour of carrying me. 'You'll not be dull, Jem,' she said; 'I'm loth to leave you.'

'Dull!' why, I am never dull, missus,' he said. 'I'll have the fellow to that there doll finished before you come home.'

Another like me? No, no! I knew full well that I was matchless, but I had no tongue to tell him so, and we left him to his vain task. A cloth was spread over our heads, and the woman took us up, saying, 'I am going, then, Jem! I'll do the best I can, and I'm sure the work deserves it! I hope the young ladies will come down. Miss Annie, she's sure to buy something for old sake's sake, else I'd never leave ye for so long, Jem.'

'Nonsense, missus,' said Jem; 'you wouldn't miss Donwell feast and the sight of Miss Annie, not for pounds, and ye knows it. So get along with ye, and come back light in the basket and heavy in the pocket.'

He laughed, and she gave him a kiss, and I never saw him again; but I must say I never saw anyone more cheery and kindly than that good man, always lying in his little bed in the corner of his room.

When I saw daylight next, it was under a tree, taller and larger than my parent, but not fruit-bearing. It was in the midst of a village green, with canvas booths around, filled with toys of all sorts, sweets, gingerbread, nuts, apples, poor wretched things compared with our old ones. Numbers of the human race were moving about, laughing, talking, screaming, shouting; there were louder cracks, shrieks of Punch, blasts of penny trumpets—enough to distract one. The good woman took her seat, set her basket down, and put all in order. I had slipped down on the journey, and an insolent monkey had fallen across my lap; but she set me up, so as to display me to the best advantage in the midst of my court. But taste was not good under that tree! Little mean-looking dolls were carried away by dirty children— —even that monkey went off, whisking over his stick, and giving me an impudent glance of triumph. I actually heard one low creature say, 'Well, I never! What a guy you've got there, missus!' However, I did not let my spirits sink, for I knew real excellence is never appreciated by the vulgar, and—had I not heard that the young ladies were sure to come?

Presently I heard a voice say, 'Oh, there she is! How do you do, Mrs. Brown? Always at Donwell feast. How's your husband?'

While Mrs. Brown was talking about her Jem, I saw two young girls and an elderly person standing by us. One had a little face rather like a new wax doll, the other was taller and plumper, with yellow hair, and she talked faster and more merrily than any one I ever heard.

'Now, what have you got for us?' she cried. 'Oh, look, look, Bertha, did you ever see such a likeness?'

'What likeness?' said the other. 'Do you mean that doll—the beauty? She really is like Maud.'

'Exactly! You see it too! The mild look of contempt, the supercilious mouth! Oh, delicious! Did your husband paint that, Mrs. Brown?'

'Yes, Miss Annie. He've got a very pretty taste of his own, has Jem, and that doll is as good a piece of work as ever he did.'

'A real work of art!' exclaimed Annie.

And for once I felt that justice was done me.

I heard the clink as I was paid for, not in trumpery silver, but handsome heavy coppers, and I was daintily taken by the waist, not wrapped up, for Miss Annie said she could not have my charms hidden. I believe she bought all that Mrs. Brown had left in her basket, and a great deal besides. Most of it she gave away to the little children who thronged about her, but she would not part with me on any account, and through all her laughter she held me fast.

'Oh, what fun we have had,' said Bertha at last, as we left the fair. 'What a pity poor Maud's back ached too much for her to come.'

'Her back ached no more than her likeness does,'

said Anne, tossing me in the air. 'It's the affectation ache!'

'For shame, Annie!'

'See whether it aches if the boys come home in time to play at lawn tennis. No, no, it was only that she was too grand to come to the village feast with us and Nurse.'

I was enchanted to hear that I was to be presented to a lady not only my rival in personal graces, but with the same refinement and contempt of the vulgar. It was still more interesting to learn that I was to be named after her, Patty.

'But is not her name Maud, if it is not Matilda?' asked Bertha,

'Not a bit of it,' returned Annie. 'She is plain Martha. She used to be Patty as a little girl, then next time I saw her, it was Matty, and now she has turned into Maud. She has it on her writing paper. I hate such humbug!'

They laughed again. I always observe that I am greeted with peals of merriment, and I smile benignantly. I like to make people cheerful.

By-and-by we passed through a park and a garden, and coming into a house, found on the sofa, in the state in which poor restless mortals most approach our serenity, the person who was compared to me. There was a resemblance. We had the same round face, pink complexion deepened to damask on the cheeks. The mouth was wider than mine, but she used to purse it up in imitation, and the waist less taper, but, as I found, she did her best to remedy that defect. Annie began to prop me upright at the opposite end of the sofa, making ripples of giggling, which awoke the sleeper, crying, ' Annie, what are you about ? '

'Installing your double, my dear,' said Annie. 'Miss Matty, let me introduce Miss Patty,' and she bent me forward so as to make a gracious bow.

'We said we would bring you a fairy,' said Bertha.

' That hideous thing ! ' she cried.

I was cut to the heart, but I smiled serenely on.

'You don't know yourself! She's your very image. Everyone was struck by it.'

Matty's answer was to snatch me up, and hurl me from her ; then jumping up she stalked out of the room, while Annie ran to pick me up, smoothed my ruffled dress, and composed my outraged feelings by saying :

'Never mind, my dear, you were too much for her feelings.'

'Really she is comically like!' said Bertha. ' I shall never be able to help laughing when Maud has done herself up to perfection, and pulled her broad, honest face into that prim look as if she had been saying, "Papa, prunes and prism," hoping everyone will think her grown up, and come out.'

'This doll shall do a work upon her!' said Annie in a solemn voice, carrying me off.

I was consigned to darkness till evening came, and candles were lighted in a large room with two little white beds, and a door opening into a smaller room with another bed. I found that the house was crowded with a large family party, and that the three girls—I think they called one another cousins—were sharing these rooms. They were going through that troublesome process which comes of not having one's clothes comfortably sewed on, once for all, like mine, though, by-the-by, there lived upstairs some dolls who were so affected as actually to be undressed every night, and who had beds of their own. They might as well be human beings—indeed they are nearly as soft and perishable. One is perfectly shocking; she wears no clothes, and is always bathing, and another makes a weak-minded little squeak when she is pinched. Perfectly disgusting!

To return to my adventures. Matty plaited her hair in two long plaits, and after going through a good deal more trouble, washed her hands (which were nearly as plump and red as mine) in some milky-looking stuff, and then drew on a pair of gloves.

At that moment Annie whisked up to her bed, and while she was not looking, placed me snugly on the soft, white pillow, covering me with the sheet, all but my head. Scarcely had I begun to enjoy this delicious repose when Matty, clad in white, hands and all, turned back the clothes, and lay down, but no sooner did she touch me than with a loud scream she bounded out of bed, crying, 'A frog! Oh, I declare I'll tell my aunt!'

Annie and Bertha were meantime making the oddest of noises and contortions, dancing about with bare feet in their night-dresses, with their hair flying; but when Matty caught up a loose red wrapper, and was putting it on, they seized her and made her look into the bed, when, I grieve to say, she demeaned herself by calling me 'that nasty thing,' and throwing me to the far corner of the room, where I fell headlong into a huge lake of water, into which I sank at once. Annie flew after me, fished me out and comforted me. 'Poor little Patty! did your namesake and likeness call you bad names and want to drown you, though you have got such nice gloves on to make your hands dainty and white?'

'I only hope she is done for!' said Matty, savagely, and she retired into bed, under the clothes.

But Annie's attentions to me were more tender.

She spread me out to dry upon a white cloth before she went to bed, and got up very early in the morning to attend to me, taking off my blue-rose dress, which had been made distressingly limp by my plunge and dressing me afresh in a blue and white stripe, with a huge bunch behind, just like Martha's, and then she added some coils and braids of hair to my head, so that I cut a wonderfully fashionable appearance by the time a great bell sounded, and Bertha and Matty began to dress themselves. Presently Matty came to the table, where lay what looked like a last year's bird's nest, and after brushing her own hair, she put this upon her head, and covered it with a great broad plait that also lay on the table. She must have wished to nail it on safely like mine, but her poor soft brains could not bear that sensible treatment, and she skewered it on with pins till she made her head look quite top-heavy.

Just as she had put on her dress and come for a last look at the glass, I was placed in front of it, looking full at her with my most encouraging and benignant gaze.

'Annie? you wretch!' she cried! 'that fright!'

'I wonder you have not more regard for yourself than to call her a fright.'

'It really is too bad! You mean to drive me distracted? I do think it is very unkind of you.'

'What, when it is your great object to make yourself her living image?'

'Living nonsense!' cried Matty, redder than ever.

'Exactly so,' said Annie, laughing. 'Now, Matty, you must know that this is your fetch, and whenever you are worshipping that idol of yours she will appear to you.'

'I'm sure I don't know what idol you mean.'

But another great bell rang at that moment, and Annie threw me into a big box, in company with a hat and a bonnet, and they all ran away.

I came forth several times more. Once, when Matty was striving and straining to pinch in her waist to be as delicate as mine, I was made to pop out on the dressing-table before her; and another time, when she had, as she thought, very secretly obtained a bottle of some mixture to improve her complexion, she found me serenely seated on the largest sponge on her washing-stand.

She was alone then, and though I smiled up in her face undauntedly, she looked so vindictive that if I had had a heart, it would have quailed in my protector's absence. There was no fire, happily for me, and she was a good creature, after all. She would not do me any bodily harm, but she opened a very black closet, and climbing up to the topmost shelf, laid me there, muttering as she did so, 'There! nobody will find you out. I hope you are buried in oblivion, you monster!'

She was scarcely gone before another step was heard. Annie was not the girl to leave me to her mercy. She had been watching all the time, and in another minute, she had rescued me from the gloom of oblivion, whatever that means, and was caressing me. 'So! did she think she had disposed of you, my dear? No, no, we know better! You shall haunt her yet! Ah! I have an idea!' And Annie began to caper about, first on one foot, then on the other, hugging me all the time.

Then she took me downstairs into the kitchen. My fears were excited lest I should be condemned to low company, perhaps to be the slave of some cottage child; but my fate was far more distinguished. I found myself laid in a deep, smooth, shining dish, while Annie took some white pasty stuff, and roofed me in with it so that I was all in the dark, except for a few little holes at the top. What next? thought I. Have they taken me for one of my own apples? I know apples go into pies, but dolls, never! I listened for some hint as to what was to become of me, but could make out nothing but tittering, and now and then, 'O Miss Annie, don't, pray!' 'O Miss Annie, you are a one!' Presently my dish was snatched up, then all was dark, an iron door was shut, and there was a terrible dull roaring all round, while it grew hotter, and **hotter, and hotter**, so that if I had had a crazy human constitution, I must have died under it. At last the door again opened, and I heard Annie exclaim, 'That's my pie! Hurrah for my *pâté*! Oh, lovely!' with more of the same kind, in the midst of which Bertha said, 'How will you get her to cut it?' 'Oh, Matty will eat anything that has a French name, because she thinks it a grown-up thing to do. She quite deserves it, for now she thinks her counterpart is gone she has broken out more ridiculously than ever with her hair frizzed out, and her Alexandra limp, and all her most unnatural airs! She must have another lesson!' Then presently I heard Annie directing the parlour maid, 'Bring it in at dinner, Jane, and take care you put it just before her, wherever she sits, and just whisper to her it is *pâté à poupée.*'

'Patty a puppy,' repeated Jane. 'She won't like that, Miss Annie.'

Annie laughed convulsively, as she gasped out an exclamation by which I understood that *poupée* is the name for my French sisters; but Jane exploded so whenever she tried to say *pâté à pup-pup-p-p-p-p-p*' that they gave up the attempt to teach her.

I heard the clatter of knives and forks, and knew that eating and talking were going on. I heard Matty's voice, saying, 'Oh, I am quite an enthusiast in the hunting field,' and Annie's voice breaking in, 'Very odd when you can't ride.'

But the crisis was coming. I felt myself set down on the table, Maud's voice was closer to me. She was saying in a low confidential tone, 'Dear Annie is so very unconventional.'

'Matty, will you cut that *pâté?*' said Annie's voice, breaking in.

'Shall I offer you some?' said Matty. 'I don't know what it is.'

'Oh, it is a new receipt—a French one,' said Annie; '*pâté à poupée,*' hurrying over the words, so that Matty serenely said, '*pâté à poisson,*' and as already four sharp spikes and a steel blade had come through my roof, a three-cornered piece was removed, and a spoon was inserted, while Matty began, 'Shall I send you some *pâté à poisson?* What fish is it?—ah—ah—ah —ah—h!'

'A maid, I should say,' observed one voice, as I sat where Matty had raised me, gazing tranquilly out on the party from the open piece of pie, wondering to see everyone shaking with laughter. There were full sixteen of them round the table, and they all vied with one another in applauding me—all save poor Matty, who was so jealous of the attention I received, that she bit her lip, the tears came into her eyes, and at last she pushed back her chair and ran away.

x

That was my great triumph, but my last. Annie and I were alone together, and she was praising me and settling my skirt after my sojourn in the dish, when the gentle voice of one of the really grown-up people broke on us: 'My dear, are not you carrying the joke a little too far?'

'Oh, mother, it is such fun!' said Annie.

'But is it kind fun, my child?'

'I only do it for Matty's good—to laugh her out of her ridiculous affectations. Whenever she does anything humbugging or nonsensical her double appears —not otherwise.'

'If it were a laughing matter to her, I would say nothing, though it is well not to make game of people too long or publicly; but do you think it hospitable or generous to torment and ridicule your guest, who has not been carefully brought up?'

Annie grew red and had tears in her eyes as she said, 'I did not mean unkindness, mother.'

'No, my child; but high spirits betrayed you.'

'I'll not do it again, mother,' she said, kissing her. 'Patty, my dear, your mission is over! I'll put you by for the next Christmas-tree.'

I am sure she sighed—I think she dropped a tear —as she laid me up in a drawer, in dread of the slavery to which I might be any day consigned.

My merits, however, have won a nobler fate. I

don't know whether I was forgotten; I only know that I was untouched for a very long time—years, I think—and that when first I saw the light again I heard a well-known voice say, 'There she is, the dear old thing!—Patty herself!' and it was Matty who uttered the cry, and held me up—Matty, taller, older-looking; I fear much less like me than in former times.

'I am ashamed to remember how I teased you with it,' said Annie, who looked older also, but less rough, though quite as merry and downright.

'My dear, nothing ever did me so much good,' said Matty. 'It was the first lesson I ever had against my vanity and conceit. What an affected little wretch I was! Yes, I know I was very cross, but it worked afterwards. Dear old Patty! May I keep her, Annie, she will put me in mind of the folly of it, whenever I am relapsing? Ah, Patty, you have the same prim, self-complacent, pursed-up mouth as ever, as if you thought yourself a paragon of paragons, just as I did three years ago. But if a doll can't improve, a girl may.'

So my triumph is complete and acknowledged. A girl may improve, for she belongs to poor human kind, but I, the true youth's companion, am a nobler, more unchanging being, perfect from the first, and incapable of improvement.

A HOLIDAY ENGAGEMENT;

OR,

THE CAMPBELLS ARE COMING.

DRAMATIS PERSONÆ.

MR. DEANE, 35 St. Clement's Road.
ROBERT DEANE, his son, clerk in a London Office.
MRS. DEANE.
ALICE } her daughters.
EDITH
MR. DEAN, 53 St. Clement's Road.
MRS. DEAN.
MISSY } her daughters.
PUSSY
MISS CAMPBELL, a governess.
MARY CAMPBELL, engaged to Robert.

SCENE: *drawing-rooms of No. 35, and No. 53.*

The change of scene might be managed by altering the table ornaments and shifting a screen, or curtain with a window painted on it.

A HOLIDAY ENGAGEMENT; OR, THE CAMPBELLS ARE COMING.

ACT I.

SCENE I.—*Drawing-room of No. 35 St. Clement's Road; 5 o'clock tea-table.* MRS. DEANE, ALICE, EDITH.

MRS. DEANE.

Was that papa's knock? I wish he would come in. How awkward!

ALICE.

Never mind, mamma. Mary Campbell may prefer taking us by instalments.

MRS. DEANE.

Poor child, it is most trying for her that Robert should not have been able to bring her down.

ALICE.

We shall have the better chance of making friends with her.

EDITH.

I wish I had gone to meet her instead of sending that stupid Alfred, whose brains have run to buttons.

MRS. DEANE.

I could not let you renew your cold before the ball. Still I almost wish I had sent you. It might have been a little less formidable for the poor girl.

EDITH.

To descend alone and unsupported on the family of her lover! Yes, it is an awful undertaking.

ALICE.

And she so shy! Hark!

Enter servant announcing MISS CAMPBELL.

MRS. DEANE (*embracing her*).

My dear! I am glad to see you. Mr. Deane was so sorry to be called away, but here are the girls.

MISS CAMPBELL (*embracing them*).

I hope soon to know you better, my dears. They are taller than I expected, Mrs. Deane.

[ALICE *pours out tea and gives it.*

MRS. DEANE.

Papa was greatly vexed at being prevented from meeting you at the station. I hope the page made himself useful, and saved you all trouble.

MISS CAMPBELL.

Thank you, Mrs. Deane, I am an old traveller.

MRS. DEANE.

It was so unfortunate that dear Robert could not come down with you.

MISS CAMPBELL.

Your son? I should have been glad to be of any service.

ALICE.

It was very good of you not to wait for him, and come down to-morrow too much tired for the ball.

MISS CAMPBELL.

A juvenile ball, my dear?

EDITH.

What, did not that foolish fellow tell you all about it? How dreadful!

ALICE.

Far gone in indifference to all sublunary matters!

MRS. DEANE.

Hush, my dear girls! Mary looks quite bewildered. She is not used to such rattles, and indeed we ought not to have trusted to him. I fear you have brought no dress, my dear?

MISS CAMPBELL.

I never supposed one would be required.

MRS. DEANE.

Never mind; Edith shall contrive your equipment. She is a good dressmaker spoilt.

MISS CAMPBELL (*stiffly*).

If I had understood——

ALICE.

It was all the fault of that foolish boy. You must punish him well.

MISS CAMPBELL.

That is not a pleasant commencement for our connection. Surely inadvertence may be excused the first time.

ALICE.

You must not spoil him. We trust to you for keeping him in order.

MISS CAMPBELL.

That was hardly a part of my specified duties.

ALICE.

What model submission!

MRS. DEANE (*hastily*).

Hush, Alice! My dear Mary, if you will not take another cup of tea, you will like to see your room.

MISS CAMPBELL.

Thank you, but pray do not trouble yourself, Mrs. Deane. If one of the young ladies would kindly show me the school-room.

MRS. DEANE.

Certainly. Young people can get on best together.
[*Exeunt* EDITH *and* MISS CAMPBELL.

ALICE.

Young people!

MRS. DEANE.

Allow something for a lover's eye, my dear. Besides, we see her at a disadvantage after her journey.

ALICE.

The journey of life, as it seems. She must have set off nineteen and arrived thirty-nine, like the people who go to sleep in fairy land.

MRS. DEANE.

So strange, too, that Robert should not have mentioned the ball!

ALICE.

He must have been afraid. She is clearly of the sort that despises such formalities.

MRS. DEANE.

Poor dear boy! He ought to have prepared us. Then we would have had her later, in Lent perhaps.

ALICE (*laughing*).

For penance! O mother, who is severe now?

MRS. DEANE.

Hush, Alice! No doubt she is highly estimable, and her travelling dress may be very disfiguring, but I own that I am astonished!

ALICE.

Above all when he declared that she was a regular kitten, ready to play with us.

EDITH (*entering*).

I'm annihilated! I've had such a snub!

ALICE.

You look as if she had boxed your ears.

EDITH.

Metaphorically she has. She told me that Mrs. Deane was at liberty to call her what she pleased, but she could not permit herself to be called Mary by me. She had not been used to it.

ALICE.

What are we to call her? La Signora Donna Maria?

EDITH.

I never stopped to ask! I made a low curtsey and ran away!

MRS. DEANE.

My dear Edith, I am so sorry! You misunderstood. Robert said she was always called Molsie at home, and no doubt she wishes you to take it up.

EDITH.

Catch me!

MRS. DEANE.

Now, girls, I entreat you not to take offence too easily at little eccentricities of manner. Remember, she is a stranger, just off a long journey, and that's a trying position. Weariness makes people look haggard, and excess of bashfulness affects the manner. Do not let us try to judge of her by this first evening, or we shall repent it all our lives. [*Exeunt.*

SCENE II.—*Drawing-room at No. 53.* MRS. DEAN, MISSY, PUSSY.

MRS. DEAN.

Take care, Pussy! What will Miss Campbell say to such attitudes?

PUSSY.

Please, darling mother, let us be comfortable till our six weeks of durance vile begin.

MRS. DEAN.

Idle child, you show how much you want a governess.

MISSY.

It is so late, I think she must have missed her train. What fun that would be!

PUSSY.

No such good luck! There's the 'bus.

MISSY.

You'll never venture to call it anything but an omnibus again.

PUSSY.

There's the door bell! the knell of our freedom and peace.

MISSY.

Only for six weeks.

PUSSY.

Holidays the wrong way for us, like 'Through the looking-glass.'

MRS. DEAN.

Silence, my dear child! There, she must be on the stairs! You can't be less frightened than I am. Ought I to kiss her, I wonder?

Enter maid announcing MISS CAMPBELL. MARY *runs confidingly up to* MRS. DEAN, *and the two girls and they all embrace.*

MRS. DEAN.

Good morning—evening. I mean. I hope you had a pleasant journey and no difficulty in finding your way here?

MARY.

Not much, thank you. There was a good-natured porter who advised me to take the 'bus, after I had extricated my boxes from a Buttons who laid violent hands upon them.

PUSSY.

O that must be the ridiculous Buttons that lives opposite, and gives himself such airs.

Enter MR. DEAN.

MRS. DEAN.

Mr. Dean—Miss Campbell.

MR. DEAN.

I am glad to see you, Miss Campbell. I hoped to have been able to meet you, but I was detained till too late. I hope it caused you no inconvenience.

PUSSY.

The absurd tiger opposite tried to run away with Miss Campbell's things, papa!

MR. DEAN.

Mischievous beast of prey! I find too that the family there are named Deane, so that we may prepare for many more encounters.

MARY.

I saw him—your son—just before I came away.

MRS. DEAN.

Indeed! Where?

MARY.

At the station. He sent his love, and said he would not fail.

PUSSY.

Dear old fellow! Of course not.

MRS. DEAN.

I am sure Miss Campbell is tired. My dears, you had better take her to the school-room. You will find tea there, Miss Campbell, and then I hope you will join us at dinner to-day at seven.

MARY.

Thank you. [*Exit with the girls.*

MR. DEAN.

What a pretty young creature!

MRS. DEAN.

What could your sister have been thinking of?

MR. DEAN.

She is very lady-like and prepossessing.

MRS. DEAN.

That's all that gentlemen heed! I might as well have another child in the school-room.

MR. DEAN

The young generation have outrun the old in science, language, and all the rest of it.

MRS. DEAN.

That is not what I want so much as a sober, staid person to look after the children and walk with them when I am engaged.

MR. DEAN.

Can't she walk?

MRS. DEAN.

So can the baby.

MR. DEAN.

If you wanted age and experience you should have told Harriet so.

MRS. DEAN.

Exactly what I did! She assured me she had just what I wanted—a person about forty.

MR. DEAN.

Youthful looks—!

MRS. DEAN.

Nonsense! I doubt if this girl is twenty. I must find your sister's letter. [*Turns over letters in a basket.*

'Experienced woman, best families, can send up gravy-soup.' No, No. 'About eighteen—objects to twice-cooked meat.' No, that's the scullery maid.

What are servants coming to? But I am sure I told Harriet I must have a superior person, able to restrain the girls and form their manners, but not too old.

MR. DEAN.

Not too old—precisely.

Enter the Girls.

MISSY.

Oh! Mamma, she is a regular duck!

MR. DEAN.

There's an opinion for you!

PUSSY.

We are to call her Molsie.

MRS. DEAN.

What do you think of that for a governess?

MISSY.

She calls us her dear little sisters, and says we shall be awfully jolly together. What is papa laughing at?

MR. DEAN.

Was that what she said, Missy?

MISSY.

Perhaps it wasn't quite, but it came to the same thing.

PUSSY.

And she has the loveliest dress, all white tulle, done up with white jessamine and lady grass.

MISSY.

And a wreath of white jessamine with lady grass.

PUSSY.

She said white jessamine was Bertie's favourite flower.

MRS. DEAN.

What should she know about Bertie?

MR. DEAN.

As a *protégée* of Harriet's, no doubt she has met him in her house.

PUSSY.

She made quite sure that he is coming home tomorrow, and cannot believe he is not to be here till Thursday.

MRS. DEAN.

What difference can it make to her? A great boy of fifteen! He will not be one of her pupils.

MR. DEAN.

If she can induce him to turn his attention to modern languages, I shall be very grateful to her.

MRS. DEAN.

Indeed I cannot have him loitering about the school-room. My object is to have the children safely kept out of mischief while I am engaged with our visitors. Miss Campbell does not come either to share the gaieties or to play with Bertie.

MR. DEAN.

Poor young thing!

MRS. DEAN.

It is what she undertook—a holiday engagement—and I shall make it plain that I can have no nonsense. [*Exeunt.*

ACT II.

SCENE I.—*Drawing-room at No 35.* MRS. DEANE, MISS CAMPBELL, ALICE, EDITH, *coming in from dinner.*

MISS CAMPBELL.

Is that your drawing, my dear?

EDITH.

Do you see any likeness?

MISS CAMPBELL.

I should have taken it for a much younger person.

EDITH.

Did you think it was meant for my father? It is Bob.

MISS CAMPBELL.

There is a family likeness of course; but is it not a pity to begin on portraits before you have studied the principles of art? You soon degenerate into caricature.

EDITH.

I never went in for much more.

MISS CAMPBELL.

I trust soon to see higher aims. Have you begun study at the school of art?

ALICE.

Yes, we have drawn onions and eggs, square blocks and round blocks, till we are heartily sick of it.

MISS CAMPBELL.

I shall be delighted to see the style taught here.

ALICE.

You will never get Robert to let you go there. He growls at our doing so.

MISS CAMPBELL.

I shall not permit him to interfere with my duties to you. When does the next lesson take place?

EDITH.

To-morrow, but of course we do not go; Robert will be coming, and there will be the ball.

MRS. DEANE.

For which we must fit you out, Mary, so that here will be no time to spare.

MISS CAMPBELL.

Do you attend the ball, Mrs. Deane?

MRS. DEANE.

Certainly; I had looked forward to introducing you.

MISS CAMPBELL.

If my presence be not needed as an escort, I should be glad to be excused. Gaiety is not in my line and unfits me for my duties.

MRS. DEANE.

I should never think of *requiring* anything. You will do exactly as you please.

Enter MR. DEANE.

EDITH.

Coffee, papa?

MR. DEANE.

Thank you. Well, Mary, I hope you will soon feel at home with us. Did you leave your mother quite well?

MISS CAMPBELL.

Thank you, Mr. Deane, as well as she ever is. She is a great sufferer.

MRS. DEANE.

Indeed! I was not aware of that.

MISS CAMPBELL.

She hardly knows what ease means.

EDITH.

Fancy! I thought she went about everywhere!

MISS CAMPBELL.

She has tried many places in vain, but no change seems to relieve her.

MRS. DEANE.

Is anyone with her?

MISS CAMPBELL.

My sister never leaves her.

EDITH.

I did not know you had a sister.

MISS CAMPBELL.

She is quite devoted to my mother and never leaves her day or night.

MRS. DEANE.

I had no notion of this! I am very sorry.

MISS CAMPBELL.

You are very kind. [*Taking up a book.*] 'The Unseen Universe.' Have you read it, my dears?

EDITH.

It is so stiff!

MISS CAMPBELL.

But well worth pains and patience. If it be too advanced a study at present, we might work up to it through 'Light Science for Leisure Moments.'

ALICE.

Suppose I have no leisure moments for light science!

MR. DEANE.

You are thinking my little girls very frivolous beings.

MISS CAMPBELL.

Perhaps they prefer languages to science; in which case I shall be happy to assist them. What have you been reading lately in German?

EDITH.

I detest German far too much to touch it.

MISS CAMPBELL.

May I ask what you have read?

EDITH.

What was the last, Alice? 'Cometh up as a Flower' or, 'The World she awoke in'?

ALICE.

Do you ever touch anything so trumpery?

MISS CAMPBELL.

Never in the school-room. I do not wonder you have a distaste for what is really improving.

MR. DEANE.

Just what I am always telling these foolish girls. I wish you would give them a taste for something better.

MISS CAMPBELL.

I will do my best, Mr. Deane, but I fear there is little opportunity in so short a time, especially with such distractions. Perhaps Archbishop Trench's lectures would serve to give a general view. Have you seen them?

MR. DEANE.

O, pray don't examine me! If you are not tired, perhaps you would favour us with a little music.

MISS CAMPBELL.

Certainly, Mr. Deane.

[MR. DEANE *and* EDITH *arrange the piano.*

ALICE.

Can I fetch your music for you?

MISS CAMPBELL.

No, thank you. No music seems to me really learnt if it cannot be played without notes.

[*Begins to play a difficult piece.*

MR. DEANE (*meantime*).

Wonderful execution! Robert had not prepared me for this.

ALICE.

Nor for a good deal more.

EDITH.

How shall we live through it?

ALICE.

Shall you submit to the course?

EDITH.

I leave that to Bob.

ALICE.

Can you account for the hallucination?

EDITH.

The music perhaps. Papa is quite entranced.

ALICE.

The strange fellow said she could only accompany herself in a few Scotch songs.

MR. DEANE.

Come girls, show Mary what you can do, though I am afraid it will be a great disappointment.

[*Curtain falls.*

SCENE II.—No. 53. MR., MRS. DEAN, MISSY, PUSSY, MARY.

MRS. DEAN.

Have you studied abroad, Miss Campbell?

MARY.

We spent last winter at Paris.

MRS. DEAN.

I lay great stress on a good French accent. Let Miss Campbell hear you speak French, Missy.

MISSY.

Oh! mother, may not we spend one evening in peace?

MARY.

A motion that I second with all my might.

PUSSY.

That's right! I knew you were a dear!

MRS. DEAN.

There is not much time to loiter away. You will look over their books to-morrow. No doubt you are a good German scholar?

MARY.

Not good—oh no!

MR. DEAN.

Come, mamma, I echo Missy's sentiment. No examination to-night, you must not defraud me of my song.   [MRS. DEAN *plays and sings.*

MARY.

Lovely indeed! I shall scold Bertie for not telling me how sweet his mother's voice is.

MRS. DEAN.

Now you will favour us, Miss Campbell. I have heard so much of your execution that I am longing for a piece.

MARY.

You have heard far more than I deserve. I can only accompany myself.

MR. DEAN.

We know what that means. That is just what mamma there says of herself.

MARY.

Pray don't say so! No one but your son ever liked my music.

MRS. DEAN.

I beg you will let us hear. If your music be not yet unpacked, no doubt there is something here that you know.

[MARY *shuffles over the music nervously. Shakes her head in despair at the pieces presented to her, then murmurs,* I'll fetch a song. [*And exit.*

MRS. DEAN.

That stuff and sentiment about Bertie I cannot away with.

MR. DEAN.

Nonsense, dear, a boy of fifteen!

MRS. DEAN.

Quite old enough for folly.

[MARY *returns with a music book, plays and sings with a trembling voice, almost breaking down at first, then, growing clearer,* 'My Heart's in the Highlands.'

MRS. DEAN (*meantime*).

Just what pleases a boy.

MR. DEAN.

Thank you—very sweet. Those old Scottish songs charm me. Have you any more of my old favourites?

MARY.

I have 'Charlie is my Darling.'

MR. DEAN.

There is nothing I should like so well. [*She sings.*

PUSSY.

O I do love Prince Charlie! You'll teach us that, you dear darling, won't you?

MRS. DEAN.

Hush, Pussy, don't be silly. Those Scotch ballads are pretty slight things. But I do not wish the children to begin to sing too early, but to improve themselves in classical music. I should like to hear something of that kind.

MARY.

What a goose you must think me! My cousin Flora, our clever one, went in once for a classical music society, but everyone grumbled so whenever she practised that she had to drop it.

MRS. DEAN.

A great mistake. Nine o'clock, children. Good-night! Miss Campbell, you look so tired, that I think you would prefer going up with the children.

MARY.

Thank you, perhaps it will be best.
[*Good-nights exchanged and kisses to the children.* Exeunt PUSSY, MISSY, *and* MARY.

MRS. DEAN.

What do you think now, Henry?

MR. DEAN.

That we have a very pleasant, though rather timid inmate.

MRS. DEAN.

Timid! She talked like one of the family. It was all I could do to repress her.

MR. DEAN.

As you did effectually, poor child! You brought tears into her eyes more than once.

MRS. DEAN.

She has much to learn before she knows her place. That is, if she every succeeds in being a governess.

MR. DEAN.

She is a thorough lady.

MRS. DEAN.

What can she be as a teacher? Your sister has just sent me down some spoilt pet of her own. I'll never engage another person without seeing her, and unfortunately there's no being off with her. It is a holiday engagement and for six weeks!

MR. DEAN.

She will do no harm.

MRS. DEAN.

How can I tell? She has come evidently to share in all the gaieties, and she will fill the children's heads with murmurs and repinings about dress and nonsense, when I meant them to be improved.

MR. DEAN.

So they will or may—in manners at least.

MRS. DEAN.

When she has no notion of manners to her superiors!

MR. DEAN.

You don't allow for woman's rights.

MRS. DEAN.

If she was one of those Graduates, I might put up with her forwardness for the children's sake, but she quite shuddered when I asked her if she had been up for a degree. She has read nothing, knows nothing, can do nothing. Did Harriet think I wanted a play-fellow for the children!

[*Curtain falls.*

ACT III.

SCENE I.—*No.* 35. MISS CAMPBELL, ALICE, EDITH.

MISS CAMPBELL.

You have not shown me the school-room, my dears.

ALICE.

We have none. Our brother turned us out, when I was sixteen, to make a smoking-room of ours, and we never had the ghost of one in this house.

MISS CAMPBELL.

Do you study in the drawing-room?

EDITH.

We practise here, and do our Essay Society work anywhere.

MISS CAMPBELL.

I should like to draw up some definite plan.

EDITH.

Very well. Of course you are free to do whatever you like.

ALICE.

Till Robert comes.

MISS CAMPBELL.

My engagement did not contemplate such interruptions.

ALICE.

Didn't it? It is the oddest engagement I ever heard of.

EDITH.

Robert will call us the interruptions.

MISS CAMPBELL.

Never mind Robert. My engagement is to you, not your brother.

ALICE.

That beats everything!

MISS CAMPBELL.

I never undertake male pupils, but I will enter on that with your mamma. At present, I wish to ascertain the progress you have made in order to lay out a plan of study.

ALICE.

Mary Campbell, you may do what you like with Robert, but we are not to be bullied into being learned prigs.

MISS CAMPBELL.

I must report this to your mother.

ALICE.

Do!

EDITH.

No, no, you would not come into the family to make mischief.

MISS CAMPBELL.

It is my duty to maintain my position. [*Exit.*

EDITH.

Run after her and make it up, there's a dear, or it will be most distressing for mother and Bob.

ALICE.

I'm not going to put myself under her feet.

EDITH.

Luckily she won't find mother, who is in the innermost recesses of the kitchen by this time.

Enter ROBERT. *Embraces.*

ROBERT.

Where is she?

ALICE.

Oh! Bob, dear fellow, we did not expect you so soon.

ROBERT.

I started at six. Where is she?

EDITH.

She was here an instant ago. I'll fetch her. [*Exit.*

ROBERT.

Well, Alice!

ALICE.

Well, Robert!

ROBERT.

Isn't she all I ever told you?

ALICE.

And more too!

ROBERT.

Did you ever see such eyes?

ALICE.

Such spectacles?

ROBERT.

My poor darling! She must have hurt her eyes!

ALICE.

I see! You had better confess!

ROBERT.

Confess what?

ALICE.

Your plot for terrifying us with a fearful old duenna in spectacles, who abhors balls, examines us on our studies, and pins us down to read a book about the Universe.

ROBERT.

Impossible! Molsie is full of fun, but she hasn't the cheek for that style of thing.

Enter EDITH *and* MISS CAMPBELL.

ALICE.

You have done it very well, Mary, but you had better confess.

ROBERT.

Where is she?

ALICE.

You see you are even taking him in. It has gone far enough. Take off your spectacles and drop it.

MISS CAMPBELL.

Is this deliberate insult?

ROBERT.

There must be some dreadful mistake.

MISS CAMPBELL.

I begin to think so. I was engaged——

ROBERT (*shrinking*).

But not to me!

MISS CAMPBELL (*with dignity*).

Certainly not, Sir. It was a holiday engagement to Mrs. Dean, St. Clement's Road.

ALICE.

It must be that awful boy!

MISS CAMPBELL.

The page? He accosted me by my name.

ROBERT.

Girls! It is no laughing matter. What on earth can have become of my poor darling?

EDITH.

Can she have set off?

ROBERT.

I saw her into the train myself!

MISS CAMPBELL.

May she not be with the lady who expected me? Stay, Mr. Robert Deane, if you will wait a moment, I will fetch your mother's—no, the other lady's—letter.

[*Exit.*

ALICE (*throwing herself into a chair*).

O I shall die of it! What have we not all gone through!

ROBERT.

How could you be so absurd? You should have acted at once, instead of gaping at her.

ALICE.

How were we to know? We only thought your taste peculiar.

ROBERT.

You were crazy! As if that creature could be my Molsie! You ought to have made enquiry instantly, and saved her from—I know not what.

EDITH.

Hush, Alice! Poor fellow, it is of no use to talk to him. [*Curtain falls.*]

SCENE III.—No. 53. MARY, *writing at the table.* MISSY, PUSSY, *both dressed for going out.*

MISSY.

Do come out, Mary; we want to show you our gardens.

PUSSY.

And Bertie's dear black dog.

MARY.

Presently, my dears, when I have finished my letters.

Enter MRS. DEAN.

You here still, children? I wish them to take an early walk before beginning work.

MARY.

Very well, I shall soon be ready, dears.

MRS. DEAN.

Did you not understand me, Miss Campbell? You would write better in the school-room, if you must write at all, at a time when I wish my daughters to be out of doors.

MARY.

I'll go presently, but as he—Bertie—does not come, to-day I must catch the early post.

MRS. DEAN.

Once for all, Miss Campbell, I permit no foolish intercourse with my son.

MARY (*springing up*).

O Mrs. Dean, how could you bring me here if our engagement had not your sanction!

MRS. DEAN.

It must have been a mistake, but as it is only a holiday engagement——

MARY.

Oh! do not be so cruel! It was in all seriousness!

[*Enter* MR. DEAN *with the letters, and gives one to* MARY, *and others to* MRS. DEAN.

MARY.

None from him! What can it mean? This letter can't be meant for me. It asks whether I can take charge of three little girls.

MRS. DEAN (*looking up from her letter*).

Young lady, if you are playing a trick, it had better come to an end.

MARY.

Someone must have played a cruel trick on me!

MRS. DEAN.

You do not pretend that you are Miss Campbell?

MARY.

Indeed my name is Mary Campbell.

MRS. DEAN.

Listen to what my sister-in-law, Miss Dean, writes.

MARY.

I never heard of Miss Dean.

MRS. DEAN (*reads*).

'Miss Campbell will have arrived by this time. Don't let the little maidens be daunted by her spectacles. She looks rather elderly and stern, but she is only thirty-six, though her appearance would make you think her ten years older.'

MARY *hysterically sobs and laughs.*
Ten years older—oh!

MR. DEAN.

Don't be frightened, Miss Campbell; it is plain that there has been a blunder. Compose yourself and try to explain.

MRS. DEAN.

I did not mean to alarm you. Pray try to explain. We expected a governess for a few weeks, named Campbell.

MARY.

Oh! I'm no impostor. I can't help being called Campbell. My brother is the Campbell of Glen Sennachie, and I came from London yesterday to stay at Mr. Deane's of St. Clement's Road, because I am engaged to his son. See, there is my ring. You believe me—oh! don't you?

MRS. DEAN.

Quite, my dear. I am sorry I seemed so unkind.

MARY.

I never saw any of his family, and he was to have come with me; but some business hindered him, and he was to follow this morning.

MRS. DEAN.

Not my Herbert, who is only fifteen.

MARY.

My Robert is twenty-six.

MR. DEAN.

I see daylight. A family named Deane has come to the opposite house; but as we are well known here, the omnibus naturally set you down here. I will run across, and find out whether they are expecting a Miss Campbell.

MARY.

Let me come with you.

MRS. DEAN.

No, no, you must not run the risk of more adventures. (*Exit* MR. DEAN.) Let me bathe those eyes, my dear. How cruel I must have seemed. You must have been crying all night.

MARY.

I beg your pardon, but your reception did provoke me, after the warm letters I had received.

MRS. DEAN.

No wonder. It was very absurd. Fetch some wine, Missy! I want to see Miss Campbell able to laugh before your papa returns.

MARY.

Oh! please no wine. Your kindness is all I want.

MISSY.

Then you are not going to stay with us, after all!

PUSSY.

What a horrid pity! We should have had such fun!

MARY.

I should have been a frightfully bad governess!

PUSSY.

But you were going to teach us to play at Consequences.

MARY.

Perhaps I can still do that.

[*A sudden peal at the bell. Enter* ROBERT *hastily, soon followed by* MISS CAMPBELL *and* MR. DEAN.

ROBERT.

My darling Molsie!

MARY.

Oh! Robert, Robert! Now I don't mind anything. (*They clasp hands.*)

MR. DEAN.

Here, mamma, here is your Miss Campbell.

MRS. DEAN.

I am rejoiced to welcome her.

MISS CAMPBELL.

I fear the error has caused much embarrassment. I ought to have looked at the address, but I thought myself safe in the hands of the page.

MARY.

I think I gave the number, but the omnibus man could not have attended.

MR. DEAN (*at the window*).

Are not those ladies your sisters, Mr. Deane. Let me fetch them in.

[*Exit, and enter with* ALICE *and* EDITH.

ROBERT.

There, girls—the true Mary is found.

(*Embraces exchanged.*)

EDITH.

Dear Mary, I am so glad.

ALICE.

There! I can trust my own senses once more.

MARY.

So can I! I began to believe I saw through the looking-glass.

ALICE.

Or that the manners and customs of St. Clement's Road were very peculiar. No—I mean that's what the other must have thought of us.

MRS. DEAN.

Too true of us likewise, I fear.

MARY.

Indeed you were very kind and forbearing.

PUSSY.

I do wish we could keep you! We do like you so!

MARY.

You wouldn't on better acquaintance perhaps! I might whip you!

MRS. DEAN.

You will let us have better acquaintance, I hope, only forgetting our first meeting.

MISS CAMPBELL.

I will try to prevent these little folks from too much regretting the charming lady they lose. Only I must first ask the elder Misses Deane to pardon the spirit of instruction that must have seemed most presumptuous and unpleasing.

EDITH.

And you must forgive us for being so shockingly disagreeable.

ALICE.

You see we weren't worthy of such a wise sister-in-law, though no doubt you would have done us a great deal of good.

EDITH.

Come, Mary, we must bear you home in triumph.

MISS CAMPBELL.

And exchange the boxes.

ALICE.

That miserable Buttons shall do it by way of penance.

MRS. DEAN.

I shall see you in that ball-dress to-night. What a shock it gave me! My dear, in token of forgiveness you must let me kiss you, and say how glad I am that yours is not only a Holiday Engagement!

[Curtain falls.

CHARLES KINGSLEY'S WORKS.

Collected Edition, complete in XXVIII. Volumes, in uniform binding. Crown 8vo. 6s. each.

POEMS. Complete Edition.

YEAST. A Problem.

ALTON LOCKE; Tailor and Poet.

HYPATIA; or, New Foes with an Old Face.

GLAUCUS; or, The Wonders of the Sea Shore. With Illustrations.

WESTWARD HO!

THE HEROES; or, Greek Fairy Tales for my Children. With Illustrations.

TWO YEARS AGO.

THE WATER BABIES: A Fairy Tale for a Land Baby. With Illustrations by Sir NOEL PATON, R.S.A., etc.

THE ROMAN AND THE TEUTON. Lectures before the University of Cambridge. With Preface by Professor MAX MÜLLER.

HEREWARD THE WAKE.

THE HERMITS.

MADAM HOW AND LADY WHY; or, First Lessons in Earth Lore for Children. Illustrated.

AT LAST; A Christmas in the West Indies. With numerous Illustrations.

PROSE IDYLLS, NEW AND OLD. With an Illustration.

PLAYS AND PURITANS; and other Historical Essays.

HISTORICAL ESSAYS.

SANITARY AND SOCIAL ESSAYS.

SCIENTIFIC LECTURES AND ESSAYS.

LITERARY AND GENERAL LECTURES.

VILLAGE AND TOWN AND COUNTRY SERMONS.

SERMONS ON NATIONAL SUBJECTS.

SERMONS FOR THE TIMES.

GOOD NEWS OF GOD.

THE GOSPEL OF THE PENTATEUCH; and DAVID.

THE WATER OF LIFE, and other Sermons.

DISCIPLINE, and other Sermons.

WESTMINSTER SERMONS. With a Preface.

THE WATER BABIES: A Fairy Tale for a Land Baby. New Edition. With 100 Pictures by LINLEY SAMBOURNE. Fcap 4to. 12s. 6d.

The Times says: "Altogether the volume can be recommended as something more than . . . of exceptional merit."

SELECTIONS FROM THE WRITINGS. With Portrait. Cr. 8vo. 6s.

HEALTH AND EDUCATION. Crown 8vo. 6s.

OUT OF THE DEEP. Words for the Sorrowful. From the Writings of CHARLES KINGSLEY. Extra fcap. 8vo. 3s. 6d.

DAILY THOUGHTS. Selected from the Writings of CHARLES KINGSLEY by his Wife. Crown 8vo. 6s.

FROM DEATH TO LIFE. Fragments of Teaching to a Village Congregation. With Letters on the Life after Death. Edited by his Wife. Fcap. 8vo. 2s. 6d.

GLAUCUS; or, The Wonders of the Shore. With coloured Illustrations, extra cloth, gilt edges. *Presentation Edition.* Crown 8vo. 7s. 6d.

THE HEROES; or, Greek Fairy Tales for my Children. With Illustrations. Extra cloth, gilt edges. (Gift-book Edition.) Crown 8vo. 7s. 6d.

"No English author has ever appeared in a more charming form. . . . This is not an *Édition de Luxe*, but it is that much better thing for work-a-day readers, an edition of admirable taste and most pleasant use."—*Pall Mall Gazette.*

Now ready, on fine paper, complete in XIII. Vols. Globe 8vo. 5s. each.

Eversley Edition.

CHARLES KINGSLEY'S NOVELS AND POEMS.

WESTWARD HO! Two Vols.	YEAST. One Vol.
TWO YEARS AGO. Two Vols.	ALTON LOCKE. Two Vols.
HYPATIA. Two Vols.	HEREWARD. Two Vols.

POEMS. Two Vols.

MACMILLAN AND CO., LONDON.

CHARLES KINGSLEY; His Letters and Memoirs. Abridged Edition. 2 Vols. 12s.

ALL SAINTS' DAY, AND OTHER SERMONS. 7s. 6d.

TRUE WORDS FOR BRAVE MEN. 2s. 6d.

KEGAN PAUL, TRENCH, AND CO., LONDON.

WORKS BY CHARLOTTE M. YONGE.

A Reputed Changeling. Two Vols. Crown 8vo. 12s. [*In the Press.*

Beechcroft at Rockstone. Two Vols. Crown 8vo. 12s.

Byewords: A Collection of Tales New and Old. Crown 8vo. 6s.

The Prince and the Page: A Tale of the Last Crusade. Illustrated. New Edition. Globe 8vo. 4s. 6d.

Little Lucy's Wonderful Globe. With Twenty-four Illustrations by FRÖLICH. New Edition. Globe 8vo. 4s. 6d.

A Book of Golden Deeds. 18mo. 4s. 6d. Globe Readings. Edition for Schools. Globe 8vo. 2s. Cheap Edition. 1s. Third Edition. Illustrated. Crown 8vo. 6s.

The Story of the Christians and the Moors in Spain. With a Vignette by HOLMAN HUNT. 18mo. 4s. 6d.

P's and Q's; or, The Question of Putting Upon. With Illustrations by C. O. MURRAY. Third Edition. Globe 8vo. 4s. 6d.

The Lances of Lynwood. With Illustrations. New Edition. Globe 8vo. 4s. 6d.

The Little Duke. New Edition. Globe 8vo. 4s. 6d.

A Storehouse of Stories. Edited by. Two Vols. Each 2s. 6d.

A Book of Worthies. Gathered from the old Histories and written anew. 18mo. Cloth extra. 4s. 6d.

The Population of an Old Pear-Tree; or, Stories of Insect Life. From the French of E. VAN BRUYSSEL. With numerous Illustrations by BECKER. New Edition. Globe 8vo. 2s. 6d.

Cameos from English History. Vol I. From Rollo to Edward II. Extra fcap. 8vo. 5s. Vol. II. The Wars in France. 5s. Vol. III. The Wars of the Roses. 5s. Vol. IV. Reformation Times. 5s. Vol. V. England and Spain. 5s. Vol. VI. Forty Years of Stuart Rule, 1603-1643. 5s. Vol. VII. The Rebellion and Restoration, 1642-1678. 5s.

A Parallel History of France and England, consisting of Outlines and Dates. Oblong 4to. 3s. 6d.

Scripture Readings for Schools and Families. Genesis to Deuteronomy. Third Edition. Globe 8vo. 1s. 6d. Also with Comments. 3s. 6d.

Scripture Readings. Second Series. Joshua to Solomon. Globe 8vo. 1s. 6d. With Comments. 3s. 6d.

Scripture Readings. Third Series. Kings and Prophets. Globe 8vo. 1s. 6d. With Comments. 3s. 6d.

Scripture Readings. Fourth Series. The Gospel Times. Globe 8vo. 1s. 6d. With Comments. 3s. 6d.

Scripture Readings. Fifth Series. Apostolic Times. Globe 8vo. 1s. 6d. With Comments. 3s. 6d.

History of Christian Names. New and Revised Edition. Crown 8vo. 7s. 6d.

The Life of John Coleridge Patteson, Missionary Bishop. New Edition. Two Vols. Crown 8vo. 12s.

The Pupils of St. John. Illustrated. Crown 8vo. 6s.

Pioneers and Founders; or, Recent Workers in the Mission Field. Crown 8vo. 6s.

The Herb of the Field: Reprinted from 'Chapters on Flowers' in *The Magazine for the Young.* A New Edition, Revised and Corrected. Crown 8vo. 5s.

The Victorian Half Century: A Jubilee Book. With a New Portrait of the Queen. Crown 8vo, paper covers, 1s. Cloth, 1s. 6d.

MACMILLAN AND CO., LONDON.

MESSRS. MACMILLAN AND CO.'S PUBLICATIONS.

Now Ready, Vols. I.–V., with Portraits, 2s. 6d. each.

ENGLISH MEN OF ACTION.

GENERAL GORDON. By Colonel Sir WILLIAM BUTLER.
HENRY THE FIFTH. By the Rev. A. J. CHURCH.
LIVINGSTONE. By Mr. THOMAS HUGHES.
LORD LAWRENCE. By Sir RICHARD TEMPLE.
WELLINGTON. By Mr. GEORGE HOOPER.

The next Volume to follow is:—

MONK. By Mr. JULIAN CORBETT. [In July.

_{*} Other Volumes are in the press or in preparation.

POPULAR EDITION, ONE SHILLING EACH.

Popular Edition, now Publishing in monthly Volumes (Volume I., January 1887), price 1s. each in Paper Cover, or in Limp Cloth Binding, 1s. 6d.

ENGLISH MEN OF LETTERS.

EDITED BY JOHN MORLEY.

JOHNSON. By LESLIE STEPHEN.
SCOTT. By R. H. HUTTON.
GIBBON. By J. C. MORISON.
SHELLEY. By J. A. SYMONDS.
HUME. By T. H. HUXLEY, F.R.S.
GOLDSMITH. By WILLIAM BLACK.
DEFOE. By W. MINTO.
BURNS. By Principal SHAIRP.
SPENSER. By the DEAN of ST. PAUL'S.
THACKERAY. By ANTHONY TROLLOPE.
BURKE. By JOHN MORLEY.
MILTON. By MARK PATTISON.
HAWTHORNE. By HENRY JAMES.
SOUTHEY. By Prof. DOWDEN.
BUNYAN. By J. A. FROUDE.
CHAUCER. By A. W. WARD.
COWPER. By GOLDWIN SMITH.
POPE. By LESLIE STEPHEN.
BYRON. By JOHN NICHOL.
DRYDEN. By GEORGE SAINTSBURY.
LOCKE. By THOMAS FOWLER.
WORDSWORTH. By F. W. H. MYERS.
LANDOR. By SIDNEY COLVIN.
DE QUINCEY. By DAVID MASSON.
CHARLES LAMB. By Rev. A. AINGER.
BENTLEY. By Prof. R. C. JEBB.
DICKENS. By A. W. WARD.
GRAY. By EDMUND GOSSE.
SWIFT. By LESLIE STEPHEN.
STERNE. By H. D. TRAILL.
MACAULAY. By J. C. MORISON.
FIELDING. By AUSTIN DOBSON.
SHERIDAN. By Mrs. OLIPHANT.
ADDISON. By W. J. COURTHOPE.
BACON. By the DEAN of ST. PAUL'S.
SIR PHILIP SIDNEY. By J. A. SYMONDS.
COLERIDGE. By H. D. TRAILL.
KEATS. By SIDNEY COLVIN.

_{*} Other Volumes to follow.

Now Publishing. Crown 8vo. Price 2s. 6d. each.

TWELVE ENGLISH STATESMEN.

The *Times* says:—"We had thought that the cheap issues of uniform volumes on all manner of subjects were being overdone; but the 'Twelve English Statesmen,' published by Messrs. Macmillan, induce us to reconsider that opinion. Without making invidious comparisons, we may say that nothing better of the sort has yet appeared, if we may judge by the five volumes before us. The names of the writers speak for themselves."

WILLIAM THE CONQUEROR. By EDWARD A. FREEMAN, D.C.L., LL.D. [Ready.
HENRY II. By Mrs. J. R. GREEN. [Ready.
EDWARD I. By F. YORK POWELL.
HENRY VII. By JAMES GAIRDNER. [Shortly.
CARDINAL WOLSEY. By Professor M. CREIGHTON, M.A., D.C.L., LL.D. [Ready.
ELIZABETH. By E. S. BEESLY.
OLIVER CROMWELL. By FREDERIC HARRISON. [Ready.
WILLIAM III. By H. D. TRAILL. [Ready.
WALPOLE. By JOHN MORLEY. [Shortly.
CHATHAM. By JOHN MORLEY.
PITT. By JOHN MORLEY. [Shortly.
PEEL. By J. R. THURSFIELD. [Shortly.

MACMILLAN AND CO., LONDON.

20.4.89.

www.ingramcontent.com/pod-product-compliance
Lightning Source LLC
Chambersburg PA
CBHW020231240426

43672CB00006B/485